Praise for *T.*
& The
by Rivera Sun

"In a world where despair has deep roots, *The Dandelion Insurrection* bursts forth with joyful abandon."
- Medea Benjamin, Co-founder of CodePink

". . . a beautifully written book just like the dandelion plant itself, punching holes through the concert of corporate terror, and inviting all to join in the insurrection."
- Keith McHenry, Co-founder of Food Not Bombs

"Let's all join and have our own Dandelion Insurrection. I give the book seven gold stars . . . and a huge *right on, sister!*"
- Joe Hock, OWS, March Against Monsanto

"This novel will not only make you want to change the world, it will remind you that you can."
- Gayle Brandeis, author of *The Book of Dead Birds*, winner of the Bellwether Prize for Socially Engaged Fiction

"*Be kind, be connected, be unafraid.* With this slogan of the Dandelion Insurrection, Rivera Sun beckons us to address the crises of our day with kindness, in community and from courage. With these tools, we can change the world one heart, one home, one block at a time."
- Anne Symens-Bucher, Canticle Farm

"THE handbook for the coming revolution!"
- Lo Daniels, Editor of Dandelion Salad

"This book is a treasure of a resource; it's a repertoire of nonviolence techniques disguised as a novel."
- **Michael Nagler, Metta Center for Nonviolence**

"Billed as 'Book Two of the Dandelion Trilogy,' *The Roots of Resistance* makes me hope Rivera Sun is punching out Book Three soon and perhaps, like Douglas Adams, will give us, someday, Books Four and Five of the Trilogy."
- **Tom H. Hastings, Conflict Resolution Assistant Professor, Portland State University**

"This novel is a nuanced political, moral, and emotional exploration of risks, sacrifices and rewards that a commitment to social justice can elicit in the hearts of some extraordinary people. I was frequently moved to ... linger and relish the rich emotional dynamics within such noble characters.
A memorable cognitive and emotional journey."
- **Nim Batchelor, Professor of Philosophy, Elon University**

"Rivera Sun always gifts us with usefully creative fiction. Her *Roots of Resistance* - the second novel of her Dandelion Trilogy - offers an inspiring story to help guide love-based strategic change efforts . . . . It takes a storyteller like Rivera Sun who inspires us to rise to the challenge as her characters do, because her stories tell us how."
- **Tom Atlee, Co-Intelligence Institute**

"Rivera Sun's *The Roots of Resistance* tells a story of a creative nonviolent resistance that is transforming the United States The characters give us hope of what could be in a way that seems achievable." - **Kevin Zeese and Margaret Flowers, Popular Resistance**

All of Rivera's books are available at her website
www.RiveraSun.com
and everywhere books are sold.

Enjoy the essays ...
a bit of fire & heart.

Rise and Resist

Essays on Love, Courage, Politics & Resistance
from *The Dandelion Insurrection*

Library of Congress Control Number:
2019938288

ISBN (paperback) 978-1-948016-03-2
ISBN (e-book) 978-1-948016-05-6
Sun, Rivera 1982-
Rise and Resist

This book is dedicated to
Lo Daniels & Dandelion Salad
for being the first to circulate the essays of
the Man From the North.

Other Works by Rivera Sun
Novels, Books & Poetry

The Way Between
The Lost Heir
The Dandelion Insurrection
The Roots of Resistance
The Dandelion Insurrection Study Guide
Billionaire Buddha
Steam Drills, Treadmills, and Shooting Stars
Rebel Song
Skylandia: Farm Poetry From Maine
Freedom Stories: volume one
The Imagine-a-nation of Lala Child

RISING SUN PRESS WORKS

Rise and Resist

Essays on Love, Courage, Politics & Resistance
from *The Dandelion Insurrection*

by

Rivera Sun

Table of Contents

DEMOCRACY

CLOSING

Introduction

These essays stand with one foot on either side of the dividing line between fiction and reality. For six years, I have picked up the pen of Charlie Rider, a character in *The Dandelion Insurrection,* and written the impassioned, incendiary essays of his nom de plume, the Man From the North. Through his eyes, I have examined common issues between his fictional world and our real world. With his fire and boldness, I have lifted up shared truths. With our common ground of love, I have called our hearts into action.

Charlie's world is different than ours. He writes in a time of (slightly) more obvious political and economic repression, particularly for writers and journalists. His essays are written under a pseudonym. He is hunted by federal agents who seek to silence him. If he speaks out boldly, it is because the hurdle of risk has already been leapt simply by breaking the silence of his world. He decries corporate power. He urges strategy for dismantling the hidden corporate dictatorship. He proposes solutions for the problems people face. He celebrates creative acts of nonviolent resistance. Most of all, he reminds us of love.

In times of injustice, danger, and oppression, love is an immeasurable force for good. Yet, it is often marginalized even by our allies. It is mocked as sentimental, naive, and foolish. Love is scorned as the folly of dreamers, poets, and idealists.

But, our experience contradicts these views. Love is a

motivating force for many of us as we strive for justice, respect, and dignity. It gives us courage to stand up against the forces of destruction, to speak out when we see wrong-doings, and to intervene where we see harm being done. Love gives many of us the strength to throw the fragile weight of our existence onto the scales of right and wrong, and try to tip those scales in the direction of justice. Humanity has shown its penchant for cruelty, misery, violence, and greed. Love is the only force strong enough to support us as we stare down the worst actions of our species. Love is what tips the balance of the world.

Love arises in many forms: hope, courage, determination, justice, kindness, respect. All of these are love by other names, shape-shifting to meet the demands of time and place. The Man From the North writes about love because it shines in times of darkness. If it is mocked and derided, it is largely because the forces of destruction do not want us to grasp its power. If we forget love, we stagger around weakened, stumbling through our efforts for change as if hamstrung. Charlie Rider risks the scoffing of others to speak for love because he knows its power. And he will risk his reputation to remind you of the superpower hidden somewhere within your heart.

Myths - old and new - are full of latent heroes discovering such hidden potential. The Man From the North's essays inspire us to pick it up. They challenge you to unleash the force of your love in our world.

This book contains a selection of Charlie Rider's essays. I like to think of them as a bundle of essays that might have been hidden in the sock drawer of one of the characters in *The Dandelion Insurrection*. Or perhaps these are the dog-eared favorites that one of Charlie's relatives shoved under the mattress to returned to over and over again for solace and inspiration. Or maybe this collection are the ones that people got from Tucker Jones and slipped hand-to-hand through their small town until someone accumulated them in a shoebox in the back of their closet. These words - both fiery and loving - can be read and re-read. They remain perennially relevant to both our hearts and our real-life world.

The essays of the Man From the North were originally published on the online journal, Dandelion Salad. Lo Daniels, the editor, has my deep gratitude for her unwavering support for these boundary-blurring, sporadically-written essays. They would not exist without her confidence in their relevancy to readers of both fiction and non-fiction.

The entire collection of the Essays of the Man From the North is still a work-in-progress. New essays are still emerging. They explore the social-political setting of *The Dandelion Insurrection*. They dive into the themes in the sequel *The Roots of Resistance*. They serve as part of my writing process as I sketch out the new terrain coming up in the third part of the Dandelion Trilogy. If you have yet to read the novels, give yourself a treat and pick them up. If you like the essays, you'll love the novels. You can find them on my website or any major bookseller's site.

I hope these writings bring you hope, courage, and inspiration. Some essays will speak more to you than others. Some essays will resonate deeply with those who rail against political injustice. Some essays will appeal to those searching to make change from a centered heart. Every essay will challenge someone. In their own ways, each essay is water for the dandelion that blossoms in you. In each of us lies the seed of resistance, the ground of truth, the potential for bold courage, the blazing light of love, the winds of change, and the golden dandelion of the human soul.

Go forth and shine! Blossom into love in a world desperate for the beauty of your truth. Rise and resist, my friends. A new day is always dawning.

Rivera Sun

Rise and Resist

I Want To Love
This Broken-Hearted Country

Essay One

I want to love this broken-hearted country, this land of shattered dreams and dashed hopes. I want to place my ear against the drumming cadence of our cities and hear the insistent pulse of life. I want to wander the forgotten highways of stories that run like wrinkles through our body politic.

Our nation is more than just our headlines. We are the collective sum of all our people, past and present, and as far into our uncertain future as we dare to imagine. We are our stories, sordid and sublime, humble and extraordinary. We are our conversations as we sit on our porches, or crouch on concrete stoops. We are our tragedies and horrors. We are our every newborn hope.

We are 320 million inhalations in every moment and 320 million exhalations in the next. For every breath that stops, another newborn gasps their first breath. We are all these moments of all our lives, a country of interwoven destinies, breathing in and out together. We are our cruelties and our violence. We are our kindnesses and healings. We are the joyful hitch in a happy step. We are sorrow weighing down our limbs.

I want to fall in love with my country, to remember our

saving graces while decrying our failings and injustices. I have reeled in horror at the face of our ugliness; now I long to remember the beautiful again. We are lost without the depth of our souls, the vision of our dreams, the illumination of our hope. We become hollow shells of armor, brittle and empty, fueled by the fumes of rage. The struggle for justice becomes a long, pointless march trudging through mud and darkness. This is no way to live, no way to fight, no way to strive for change.

Instead, we must sink the roots of our heart and soul into the deep earth of human existence. We must seek out the nourishing ground of love. For every cruelty tossed in our faces, we must grasp the balm of kindness, connection, courage, and caring. These are the truths we stand up for. These are the "country" that we defend - a nation without borders, a place defined by the human heart. These values are the bedrock of what we call justice: the inalienable rights of all humans to live in peace, in hope, in compassion, in a community that dares to respect and even love itself.

Our country has learned to despise itself. Some cling their race, class, and gender then shove everyone else out of their "halluci-nation" of this country. Some include everyone in the shape of their imagined nation, but sneer and degrade the ones they despise. We are a nation divided by our fears and hatred, a nation that cannot bear its truth: we are broken-hearted, battered, terrified by what we are, unable to face the mirror and look our truth in the eye.

Dare to look. Your human soul is strong enough to hold the sorrow, the pain, the shock, and the fear that stark and honest truths evoke. Hold your gaze until the "monster" you first perceive shifts, and a deeper layer is revealed. Like the old folktale of Tamlin shape-shifting through bear and beast, snake and lion, be like brave Janet, holding him in her love. Such love can weather the shape of our monstrousness until the truth of our humanness re-emerges.

We are a nation that needs to love our true selves – not the hubris of our illusions of imperialistic might. We need to discard our arrogant posturing and bullying, and see the wounds and insecurities underneath. We need to let go of our bloated and false pride. We need to love the humbler truths, the hidden stories, the wounded places needing healing. We need to love our children and our elders, our people in all their colors, our artists and our workers, our frail and strong alike. This is the foundation of meaningful change, the commitment to a love that is strong enough to heal our brokenness, to address our wounds, to speak to our simple human beauty, to remember our kindness and commonalities, and to nurture the basic human values that make us truly great. We need to believe in one another, to have faith that we – all 320 million of us – are worth the effort that healing and transformation require.

I want to love this broken-hearted country, this land of shattered dreams and dashed hopes. I want to help us rise, together, and embody our visions of equality and respect, caring and connection, justice and transformation. I want to fall in love again so that we all might heal and live and change.

Rise and Resist

The Occupied Territory
of the United States of America

Essay Two

It happened so subtly; we missed the corporate coup. Like shadows, corporations surrounded our country and slowly strangled it. They crept into Congress, the White House, the Supreme Court, the FDA, the military, the Department of the Interior: everywhere you look, a corporation controls the decisions of this nation. We have become the occupied territory of brand names, corporate logos, monopolistic power, and corporate greed.

It would be easier to understand what has happened if they wore red armbands and goose-stepped. But no, the minions of corporate power wear false smiles, carry empty promises, and fly in private jets. The less-powerful rank-and-file of the corporate state look like our neighbors, relatives, and friends. They are not our enemy. It is the destructive behaviors of the corporate state - and its occupation of our government, culture, and society - that we must rebel against.

Every aspect of our lives has become an extraction zone for the insatiable hunger of corporate greed. They take our labor, sweat, and time. They steal our work, ideas, and inventions. Their extortionist prices devour our earnings. They supplant our culture with theirs. They replace education with corporate programming. They broadcast propaganda and

11

advertisements instead of news. They pass policies and legislation that maximize profits instead of protecting people and planet. They privatize the public assets built by collective investment. They take the resources of the land and dump the costs of destruction onto future generations. They tax our earnings to fund police and military to guard their interests. They suck up our life savings through health costs that come from the toxic side effects of their greed.

The corporate state gives us back mere illusions of freedom. Behind the smoke and mirrors, empty rhetoric and false words, lies a clenching fist of control. The moment you step out of line or dare to dissent, you run smack into the invisible electric fences of their laws and police. If you stay within their boundaries, they reward you by allowing you to think you have consumer choices. Each option funds their stockpiles of wealth, but you're permitted to fantasize that you can vote with your dollars for the lesser of two evils.

We are occupied territory from sea to shining sea, from urban to rural region, from our outer edges to our inner souls. The corporate state extracts profits from every angle of our lives. To win independence requires inner, outer, and utter revolution. It demands that we put the tools of nonviolent struggle to work toward changing every aspect of our lives – social, economic, political, spiritual, cultural, mental. If we wish to end the occupation of the corporate state, we must turn our lives inside out and upside down until they serve us, and not the other way around.

Rise up. Rebel. Throw the occupiers out.

Liberty and Strategy for All

Essay Three

You must believe that pockets of resistance exist. As America plunges into darkness, some people burn with resistance like fires in the night, aglow with respect for the civil liberties that define the modern ideal of freedom. The quiet murmur of their impassioned voices will call to you as they discuss nonviolent strategy and struggle, but you will not be asked to join them until you strike the matchstick of your heart, build a fire of your determination, ignite the blaze of your courage, and reach out to others.

You must pull out those weathered, dog-eared books – the ones that you saved before the government banned them, the volumes that escaped the bonfires of the increasing authoritarianism of our corporate-controlled society. If you were not wise enough to collect these writers before our Freedom of Speech vanished without so much as a gasp of popular dissent, then you must to try and gather them now. Meanwhile, in these articles of *The Man From the North,* I will do my humble best to pass on the knowledge of how to topple tyranny from its throne.

I ask you to weigh my suggestions on the scale of your own reason. Accept nothing without examining it with the knife of your own mind. Sharpen the edge of your intellect and dissect all strategies and proposals. By this, I do not mean the opinionated arrogance that rejects all notions but one's own. (Indeed, one's own strategies must be submitted to the sharpest critique of all.) What I ask of you is to act like a good friend, one who values the thoughts of another and will acknowledge the strengths and weaknesses of his or her friend's proposal with determined compassion. The stakes are high and great wisdom is required.

We are not playing with toy soldiers or video games. Resistance is a word that encompasses human hearts, blood, sweat, tears, families with small children, the elderly, the frail, and the tender hopes and dreams of all. The fabric of society – woven from those we know and love – is on the operating table. We are surgeons with scalpels in hand, trying to remove the spreading cancer of injustice, corruption, and tyranny. Cut carefully. Casualties are not numbers; they are faces with names. People are not profits; they are the immeasurable potential of the future. This is why we must commit to struggle . . . and also proceed with great care. Be a good friend to me, and to all others: lend me your wisdom, and I will lend you mine.

Gather with others and pull out the books of those who detail the strategies of nonviolent struggle. Everything we have been taught about such struggles has been warped and twisted with falsehoods. Nonviolent struggle is not passive . . . nor is it ineffectual. It has toppled dictators around the world and succeeded more often than violent uprisings. The corporate regime that currently controls our textbooks, our newspapers, our popular media and entertainment perpetuates misinformation about such struggles. They would have you believe that Rosa Parks got tired one day and refused to give up her bus seat.

That is a lie.

Rosa Parks was deeply trained in nonviolent struggle, as were the other Civil Rights Movement activists who planned the Montgomery Bus Boycott long in advance of its eruption. This is not taught in schools, for it would empower children to know the means to end oppression. The watered-down version of Rosa Parks' story is just one example of the mountain of false perceptions that are perpetuated by the empowered elite. They fear strategic nonviolent struggle . . . and rightly so.

Strategic nonviolent struggle draws its strength from an undeniable truth: governments rule by the consent of the governed. Such cooperation may be willing or coerced, but without our support, the government cannot operate. We prop up injustice by complying with laws, providing our skills and services, showing up at our jobs, and giving tyranny the full benefit of our compliance. The American Declaration of Independence clearly outlines this, along with a call to moral responsibility:

". . . *Governments are instituted among Men, deriving their just powers from the consent of the governed, that whenever any Form of Government becomes destructive of these ends, it is the Right of the People to alter or to abolish it.*"

This time has come.

Pull your dog-eared books from hiding, and begin to study and strategize. Tyranny can - and will be – toppled. Here is how it will be done.

We must remedy our ignorance of the tools of nonviolent strategy and learn the sensible application of these tools. Let us study diligently, as if we had been asked to build a skyscraper and, not knowing whether circumstance shall call upon us to lug concrete or draft the blueprints, let us prepare for whatever may be required.

Since no blueprint for ending tyranny in our country has been shown to us, let us begin drafting many designs in small groups and then seek out others with whom we can compare notes. Acknowledging our own ignorance and lack of experience (for who among us has successfully removed tyrants from power?), let us use the assistance of others to rout out the weaknesses of our designs and revise them to increase their strength.

We must exercise caution, but not fear, as we reach out to others. Not all will be who they claim. Some will be agents of our opponents; others are bitter humans who would tear the joy from a child and trip elderly people out of spite; still others suffer from despair and in their despair would smother out all chances of success. But let us be open with our knowledge, unless, for strategic reasons, it is absolutely necessary to conceal it. Secrecy is a double-edged sword. It can suffocate resistance movements like ours that depend on broad support of the populace. Let us use anonymity before secrecy. Tack your ideas to telephone poles if you must, but do not withhold much-needed knowledge from the people. They hunger for hope. They starve for solutions. As often as possible, we should reach out and remind others that resistance is not only possible, it is happening in our own communities.

Using an ounce of patience and a pound of precaution could prevent a ton of foolhardy actions from causing losses of life and limb. Let us take the time to study and strategize now, so that when we move into action it can be with great certainty, commitment, and determination. All dictatorships have weaknesses. We must study the Achilles' heels of our corporate-political regime and strike wisely. They are strong and we are weak. We must use time and strategy to shift this distribution of power. Let us sway the social institutions and the populace to shift allegiance. Oppressive regimes can fall quickly, but only when their pillars of support have been eroded through persistent resistance.

We can plan for success by crafting not just a blueprint of strategy, but also a vision of what should follow. Such a vision for the future should evoke not just our long-buried, wild dreams, but also our nuts-and-bolts pragmatism. Without a well-crafted plan, the power vacuum opened by our struggle may be quickly filled by a coup d'état or an even harsher regime.

This last may prove equally – if not more – challenging than strategizing a plan of resistance. In a nation as diverse as our own, the desire to be free of tyrannical control may be widely shared, but the vision of a better world will take many shapes and forms. Compounding our differing views is a legacy of dispute. We, the people, carry many layers of prejudice and suspicion that the elite – both liberal and conservative – has fostered in us. But, since our arguments and dogmatism serve to their advantage, let us remove that source of their power by reviving the art of respectful discourse. If we seek our liberty from tyranny, we must exercise both the rights *and* the responsibilities of a civil, democratic society: the right to speak *and* the responsibility of listening; the right to our beliefs *and* the responsibility to allow others their views; the right to work toward our goals without fear of violent repression *and* the responsibility of ensuring that same freedom even for those with whom we disagree.

This list goes on. With liberties come responsibilities, for

17

human beings are an interconnected species, and true freedom is found not in isolation, but in concert with others. At times such as these, the deep strands of our connections weigh heavily. Tyranny binds cruelly with the weight of unjust laws and state-sanctioned violence. But, by working together to articulate a strategy for liberation and a vision that encompasses our rights and responsibilities to each other, we can lift the iron shackles of oppression and break free. Together, we can create a civil society that respects freedom for all without sacrificing the rights of the many for the privileges of the few. Such liberation has been achieved in other countries. It will be achieved in ours. So, get out your books, gather some friends, and let's get to work.

Emergence:
Revolution Within and Without

Essay Four

A self-organizing movement like the Dandelion Insurrection relies on the collective and individual capacity of our participants. We are only as strong as the synergistic sum of our parts. The weaknesses of each person affect the effectiveness of the whole movement. The wisdom or folly of every individual contributes to either the intelligence or foolhardiness of our shared strategies and decisions.

Everything matters to this equation – our short tempers, hard won experience, creativity, grounded awareness, our respect for one another – and most of all, our knowledge of nonviolent action as the tools of change with which we are dismantling injustice and building a new world.

It matters because of the nature of our movement. The Dandelion Insurrection did not emerge from a single point. We never had a solitary leader or central command. It began by following the actions of ordinary people, telling their stories, and weaving a web of awareness about the dispersed resistance that was growing. We marked a map full of pushpins and described it as an insurrection. The dandelion grew up as a symbol . . . people started using it, and thus, the Dandelion Insurrection emerged.

Emergence is the jaw-dropping, beautiful arising of complex systems in an ever-changing, interconnected world. It is as old as the origins of life in the primordial soup. It is as enduring as each chapter of evolution. It unfolds daily, moment-by-moment in every plant, animal, and ecosystem. It blossoms in each one of us. Whether the powerful like it or not, it is at work in the very systems of economics and politics they are trying to dominate and control. It is entwined in the practices of real, participatory democracy - and in nonviolent movements for change.

Emergence has been the co-creative mechanism of the story of the world since the dawn of time. And, if humanity wishes to have a future on this planet, we will need to get cozy with emergence.

In the work of reconnecting with the emergent nature of our world, the Dandelion Insurrection serves as both training ground and mechanism of transformation. We are the means of eternity in the making. We have planted our seeds in the ground of existence. Our roots stretch into the very same soil from which all that we know has grown. We are organizing in alignment with the vast processes of the universe. When one participates in the Dandelion Insurrection as one of the participatory members of this leaderful movement, one must unlearn old behaviors of dominator culture and relearn the practices of being human, being real, and being a part of this beautiful, ever-changing, interconnected world.

The Dandelion Insurrection is a nonviolent movement that challenges and transforms injustice, domination, authoritarian control, and the corporate take-over of our government and structures of power. But more than that, we are a tidal wave of life and change sweeping through the hearts, minds, and actions of our populace. We are a process that makes participants out of subjects; people out of consumers; and human beings out of victims, oppressors, and bystanders locked in old patterns.

We are rooted in nonviolence because it is integral to this process. Violence is fundamentally based in disempowering someone, holding power over them with the willingness to cause pain to get one's way. The effectiveness of nonviolent action rests in withholding participation and cooperation, by placing our resources in new systems; and by intervening and disrupting the functioning of unjust systems. It stands upon the recognition that we are all connected to the vast ecosystems, economies, societies, and cultures that churn in our world. Whether against our will or with our willing consent, these systems rely on our continued active participation (or passive acceptance). If we, individually and collectively, shift our interaction in those systems, they also must shift and adapt to that change. The larger we make our shifts, the greater the system will feel the pressure to adapt to that change. The more strategically we can either withdraw participation or intervene in the system, the more likely that we can achieve the exact changes we desire.

Skillfulness counts . . . and because the Dandelion Insurrection is not a top-down movement with commands coming from leaders on high, the skillfulness of each person is critical to the success of the whole. Like barn raisers, we each must know how to swing a hammer and where to place the nail; when to lift and hold, and when to lower and release. There is no substitute for training ourselves. If we want an effective movement, the seeds of skillfulness must be planted in each participant.

This means you. Along with your friends, family members, and community, you must know the hundreds of methods of nonviolent action (our toolbox of tactics). You must know the basic dynamics of nonviolent struggle (the architectural principles of building change with those tools). You must know the goals that the Dandelion Insurrection collectively seeks (the sketch of the house we wish to live in). You must train to build your muscles for action. You must gather in small groups to practice using nonviolent action - this is like practicing how to swing the hammer and hit the nail on the head. Then, when we move into action, we can move with trust and respect. We know that the task we wish to accomplish is achievable. We know that the barn will be raised as safely, efficiently, and smoothly as possible. The work we do is dangerous by nature. Our skillfulness individually and collectively can be the factor that saves – or risks – thousands of lives, including our own.

There is one thing more: every emergent system – from a sprouting seed to a newborn galaxy – is guided by organizing principles. These principles shape how it is formed and the formation that it takes. They make trees green and leafy with trunks, limbs, branches, and twigs. They give fish scales, gills, and tailfins. They determine that human babies will grow up into human adults while tiger cubs grow up into tigers. The Dandelion Insurrection has four guiding principles for our actions. Take them to heart as you act as part of this movement. They have emerged along with the Dandelion Insurrection. We saw them emerging, identified them, articulated them, and adopted them consciously. They give us strength, beauty, and grace. They have served us well in the past and the present. With your participation, they will serve us well into the future we're building.

The principles:

- Nonviolence: don't cause physical harm to anyone or anything.
- Create connections: build community, open dialogues, organize action.
- Use our civil liberties of speech and assembly to stand up for democracy.
- Keep humanity and the planet alive: stop destruction; support the life affirming.

And, of course . . . *be kind, be connected, be unafraid!*

Rise and Resist

Disrupt! Interrupt!
The Ground of Resistance is Ours!

Essay Five

A smoothly functioning society is created and maintained by the people. Children go to school, workers show up at their jobs, shipments are made, groceries and purchases are bought, bills are paid, goods and services are delivered; and so on. In times of justice, when the workings of society are fair, respectful, and uphold the rights and dignity of humanity, then the people have every reason to collectively maintain functional workplaces, schools, roads, social events, and so on.

But in times of injustice, when the government, businesses, courts, and institutions are corrupt and abusive, it is the right and the responsibility of the people to deny power holders the benefit of a seamlessly operational society. Students must walk out of classes. Commuter traffic must be interrupted. Workers must strike. Shoppers must boycott. Widespread nonviolent action in the forms of noncooperation and intervention must be used to withhold the socio-political consent of our day-to-day lives.

Corrupt and abusive power holders view these actions as objectionable and abnormal. They are, however, indications of a robust and sane civil society grasping the source of its political power. The ability to give or withhold our consent or cooperation is the most important and ultimate form of checks-and-balance within our political system. It is the power most feared by the unjust, the bullies, the crooks, and the abusive for it is the ordinary, everyday strength of grandmothers and children, mothers and fathers, workers, teachers, and students.

In times such as ours - when rich people control vast monopolies, mass media, and the government - it is how we stand up to their bullying and abuse. When their concentrated control of power does not deliver decent food to our children or put solid roofs over our heads, then it is our right to refuse to give them a well-ordered society. When their domination of our governing system does not offer freedom from persecution and discrimination to every citizen; nor safety from the violence of the state, vigilantes, or others; nor affordable healthcare; nor freedom from the shackles of debt; nor an environment that can sustain and nurture life . . . when such systemic failures run rampant then it is our duty to resist the ruling elite using our ability to maintain or disrupt the functional workings of our world.

The people have no inherent obligation to deliver functional workplaces to wealthy business owners, nor profits from sales of consumer goods. We have no duty to comply with the protocols of a governing body controlled by abusive oligarchs. The people *do* have reason to respect and uphold their fellow citizens, to maintain systems and institutions that protect and benefit the public good, and to cooperate with economic systems that are fair and respectful to workers, suppliers, and consumers alike. We have every reason to grant functional systems to our brothers and sisters wherever those systems improve the well-being of all.

But at times such as these, when our society as a whole

26

serves largely to cripple, impoverish, imprison, and oppress the bulk of the populace, then the people must deeply question whether our normal, orderly days are a source of pride and contentment . . . or whether they are analogous to Christian Germans completing their shopping while the Jewish Germans were being sent to the gas chambers. Or worse, for in this metaphor, we are both the abused and the pawns of the abuser. We are the Jews who worked for the Nazis, keeping records of gold teeth, glasses, and pocket watches taken from the pockets of the condemned.

Our productive, well-ordered society is maintained by millions of people. In times of justice, this society could be a vibrantly alive and beautiful reflection of the mutual respect and prosperity of a nation at peace with itself. In times of injustice, however, such a well-behaved society is shameful, a sign of either our callous disregard for each other, or of our ingrained disempowerment and despair. Currently, it largely manifests as a massive machine of sleepwalking automatons, mindless of the effect of our actions.

The sleeping giant of our populace must awaken. The unconscious must become alert, aware, and empowered. The functionality of our daily world is the ground of our resistance to injustice. We must give or withhold our day-to-day compliance with so-called normality as a form of flexing our political muscles. With this power, we can rein in abuse and reward justice. With this power, we demonstrate the tangible will of the people to the power holders in business and government.

This is true for all political situations from dictatorships to democracies. In our times when so much is controlled by so few, we, the people, must use our socio-political strength to demand justice from the rich and powerful . . . and, even more importantly, to wrest back the institutions and systems of power from the stranglehold of oligarchs, to insist on shared power and democracy; and to unravel their monopolistic control.

We must each study our daily lives for pivot points of resistance. Every task, chore, job, appointment, errand, and social obligation . . . *everything* can become a place of giving or withholding consent. When our individual actions are multiplied by the efforts of our fellow citizens, powerful levels for making change emerge. Through these places, our yearning for justice has the potential to become embodied action. We must study our lives for our sources of power. Then we must collectively use it to protect the dignity and well-being of all.

The Tools of Nonviolent Struggle Should Never Lose Their Edge

Essay Six

The tools of nonviolent action and the skills of struggle are as vital to these times as reading, writing, and arithmetic. Training to use them is as essential as learning how to use a computer. The ability to boycott and strike is as important as the ability to drive a car or ride public transit. Every citizen who knows how to use email should also know how to protest, walk-out, shut-down, occupy, blockade, and more. This is the only way the power of the people can hold the power of oligarchs in check.

Before the oligarchs concluded that the study of civics was detrimental to the longevity of their rule, every elementary student learned about checks-and-balances. Theoretically, the legislative, executive, and judicial branches of government were supposed to hold each other in balance. It was a reassuring fairy tale for the average citizen, but it never served the average citizen. This system of checks-and-balances merely held one oligarchic faction in check with the other. Nothing in the arrangement guaranteed that the government would be responsive to the ordinary people's needs.

When oligarchs are the only ones who sit in Congress, occupy the Oval Office, and wield the judge's gavel, then it is a government of, by, and for the oligarchs, responsive only to their elite interests . . . not to ours. This has been the case since the earliest days of the formation of the United States. The Founding Fathers must have suspected that the slogan, "a government of, by, and for rich, white men" wouldn't produce the revolutionary fervor they needed to overthrow King George's colonial rule. The phrase "of, by, and for the people" sounded far more inspiring to the thousands who waged struggle with mass acts of noncooperation, importation boycotts, civil disobedience of unjust British laws, and collective refusal to pay the Stamp Tax. Many more fought and died in the Revolutionary War for an illusion of inclusion in the definition of "We, the People". The history of the United States has been one long struggle for inclusion that continues to this very day.

If we learn nothing else from our history, we should know this: the tools of nonviolent struggle should never lose their edge, gather dust, or fall from active use among the people. To gain – and maintain – a true government of, by, and for the people, all of us must grasp the considerable power of collective non-cooperation, disruption, and intervention. We must do so with regularity and with ferocity. Our own history of social justice illuminates this truth: women's suffrage was only gained through the direct action of women, African-Americans gained functional rights and equality only when they organized; workers achieved wage increases only when unions and movements went on strike.

Maintaining the common use of the tools of nonviolent struggle can be aided by adding the legal right to use them to our laws. We need a second Bill of Rights that preserves not just the right to Speech, Assembly, and Petition, but also the right to organize, strike, form unions, boycott unjust businesses, engage in collective disobedience of unjust laws, and more. Such a Bill of Rights would make evident that the demonstrated "will of the People" is respected and viewed as a legitimate political force.

Don't hold your breath waiting for this to happen. Oligarchs are unlikely to enshrine in law anything that limits their power. However, the lack of such laws should not stop the populace from using nonviolent struggle. Indeed, in the history of global movements for change, the banning or prohibition of movement activity and dissident organizing has not stopped people from rising up for justice. Many movements have circumvented the laws in order to mobilize for change. Even in places where the *knowledge* of nonviolent struggle is banned, people have circulated important literature and workshops on how to wage struggle. In Chile, citizens met in small groups to train to overthrow the Pinochet regime. In the Philippines, the Catholic Church hosted the trainings. In other places, banned pamphlets were shared at great personal risk. In Soviet Bloc nations, hidden presses printed literature about nonviolent struggle clandestinely. As long as knowledge of nonviolent struggle is essential to social, political, and human rights, people will find ways to access it.

In the end, it is the people's *willingness* to learn and use nonviolent struggle that ultimately liberates them. The absence of our willingness to use nonviolent struggle is what keeps us disenfranchised, disempowered, chained to the corrupt system, floundering for savior figures, and failing to achieve our social justice goals.

Currently, the US populace views nonviolent action as something unusual and out-of-the-ordinary. "Activists" are distinct from citizens. But if boycotts, strikes, walk-outs, and

31

shut-downs became as common as calling your senator or signing a petition, we would rapidly and effectively win major social justice advances. Nonviolent struggle is not about pleading with politicians to do "the right thing". It is not about voting the "right" people into power to do the right thing. It is about grasping the ability to noncooperate, disrupt, and intervene in the activity of a society in pursuit of tangible changes for social justice.

Nonviolent struggle empowers the people to hold all aspects of their society accountable. Nonviolent action's capacity to withdraw support, or disrupt systems of oppression, and intervene in injustice can target any institution, business, social practice or group, political party or policy, and cultural behaviors and beliefs.

Every meaningful advance for equality and justice in our nation's history, beginning with our struggle for independence, has won because it mobilized mass numbers of people to cease their participation in life-as-usual. If we wish to see meaningful changes in our lifetime, we, too, must find the willingness to pick up the tools of nonviolent struggle and construct the world of our dreams.

Baking the Bread of Revolution

Essay Seven

There is a formula for revolution. The corporate-political elite are following it to perfection: steal the money, corrupt the power, imprison the people, starve the children, poison the water, pillage the resources, enslave the workers, eviscerate justice, stalk the citizens, stifle dissent, and inject terror in the bloodstream of society.

Massive unrest and movements for social change are natural reaction to such conditions. With these ingredients, we're cooked. Either we'll revolt like cattle lunging to escape the slaughterhouse, or we will wage struggle for revolution in a process as natural as the alchemy of bread baking. It is unbelievable that the powerful don't understand: if they mix the living yeast of humans into the flour of our earthly existence, apply pressure and heat . . . poof! We will rise toward life, nourishment, and sustenance of our communities.

They're adding kindling to the woodstove and sugar to the yeast. They're kneading the dough that is our populace with every blow of injustice that they strike. Where we were once pudgy, weak, and pasty, we are growing tougher through their beatings. Our firma materia is strengthening, our elasticity toughening with tenacity. As they knock us down, again and again, we rise despite their efforts.

Fools! Do they not see? If they had left us alone, we would never have become the bread of revolution. My fellow men and women would have stayed upon the shelves, tucked into bottles and jars of our societal containers. Separated like spices on the rack, we would have stayed neatly segregated – blacks over there; browns, here; whites, there; rich expensive ingredients on the top shelf; cheap goods shoved underneath the sink.

But in their greedy hunger, the corporate-political thugs have torn apart the kitchen of our country. They devoured the cake, the éclairs, the crème-de-la-crème. They consumed the muffins, the scones . . . and now they want the bread. Addicts! They have ripped open the flour sack and forced a trembling woman to bake for them, silencing her hungry children as she labors for their greed.

But listen, well, for some things are sacred . . . and bread is one of them.

As lustful palms reach to tear apart the fresh baked bread, we will burn them. We will scald their tongue and sear their throats – not through spite, but through the nature of the bread of revolution that bakes hot and potent in the fire of their greed. Revolution is a law of human physics, a lever of society. When they push the people down, we have no choice but to rise. When they tear at the sacred bread of life; when they stuff their mouths in front of hungry children; when they reach for the last crumbs as young eyes cry . . . their mother will ignite a revolution.

And where the corporate-political powers could suppress all others, they will not stop this woman. She is a force of nature – a biological necessity – an imperative for our survival. She is beyond one person, one body, one race, culture or creed. Men and women, both, embody her powerful spirit. The woman who rises in defense of life transcends all divisions in humanity. She lives in each of us. She will rise in us, unstoppable.

In every heart, around the world, the bread of revolution is baking.

Rise and Resist

A Revolution
By Any Other Name

Essay Eight

There are some who mince their steps and words, who hush the bold and outspoken, who advise moderation. But, a revolution by any other name does not smell as sweet. *Reform* does not cut it. *Resistance* is not enough. *Massive change* is vague. *Transformation* calls to mind change, yet does not invoke the burning urgency, the gritty intensity of the tsunami of change we need. *Evolution* implies an unrealistic image of our corporate political pawns awakening, growing, and evolving.

A *revolution* casts the corporate politicians out of power and replaces them. It is specific. It is accurate. It is the word we need.

To the credit of those who urge caution in our language, there are times when a metaphor, a code word, or a subtle substitution is wise. But there are also times when horses and spades must be called by their true names. We must be brave enough to let the word we need cross our lips and be the word we mean.

Revolution. It is not a comfortable word. We must get used to it. The scope of change we need is not comfortable. So many of us cling to the familiar structures and systems, but these are the exact mechanisms of our suffering and our destruction. We need to be uncomfortable, thrown off balance, shoved out into unknown territory. For all that is known is corrupt, unjust, and dangerous. We must learn to dance in the upheaval of revolutionary times.

And, we must learn to live with revolutionaries, as much as with revolution. We have grown uneasy with such things. We are too accustomed to passivity, too accepting of abuse, too addicted to our minor comforts. We are afraid of the effort it takes to change. The dire necessity of crisis should inspire us to extraordinary greatness, yet we shrink like snails back into the shells of our individuated, permissible existences.

The revolutionary must be fearless enough to cry out that the emperor has no clothes. She must dare to live awake in the living nightmare of a crumbling and terrifying empire. He must be willing to speak honestly about the scope of the dangers. She must be visionary enough to propose solutions. They must be committed to the rigors and challenges of the journey toward change.

The revolutionary must dream outside the permitted corrals of the system. He must color outside the lines of societal definition. She must imagine the unimaginable. They must believe the impossible is, indeed, possible.

The revolutionary rejects stale myths and patriotic lies. Their loyalty is offered only to the long quest of humanity for dignity, respect, equality, justice, freedom, compassion, and peace. The revolutionary will wrench those values from the false platitudes of the powerful. She will rock the boat of the world, not the lulling cradle of the status quo. He will face the scorn of stability-loving opposition undaunted, for the revolutionary is ever tempest-tossed, laughing in the winds of the change.

The revolutionary grows lean with hunger for change, impassioned with yearning for a better world. They make the defenders of the status quo as frightened as chickens in a coop while the wolf song of revolution howls in the night.

Does this make you uneasy? Does the revolutionary spirit stir discomfort in your soul? Good. Complacency is a death sentence. We all know it. That which is comfortable to humanity today becomes the demise of our species as tomorrow dawns. Only the revolutionary spirit offers hope – and it is a hard hope, a bucket of cold water in the face of blind, drunken addiction to a destructive way of life.

These times of revolution and revolutionaries will not be comfortable. Get ready for them. They are here.

Rise and Resist

Blowing Up The Armory

Essay Nine

We have been losing ground. Corporate politics has invaded many sectors of our lives. In times of tactical retreat (in preparation for later advances), the military uses a tactic called *blowing up the armory*. It describes the act of destroying any unsecured weapons and munitions to prevent their opponents from capturing them and using the arsenal against the retreating forces.

Those of us engaged in nonviolent struggle may look around at the innocuous weapons of our pamphlets and banners and dismiss this tactic as not applicable. This, however, is a mistake. The armories of nonviolent struggle are the social institutions that maintain the status quo of civil society. A treasure trove of resources is stored within these facilities: law, education, communication, transportation, wealth, authority, governmental processes, business, commerce, transaction, regulation, media, entertainment, and much more.

We must look starkly at the flailing status of our struggle: these institutions have been invaded by corporate control and extreme greed. We no longer have the option of blowing up these armories – too many innocent civilians are entrenched inside these conquered territories. Nonviolent struggle rejects the notions of "acceptable levels of casualties". No loss of human life or causing of physical harm can be justified by the worthiness of our cause. We have never had the militaristic luxury of wanton destruction.

But neither can we be passive. The tools of our civilization are being forged into weapons of mass destruction. Our responsibility is clear. We must help citizens to safety. We must remove the arsenal from being used to cause harm to ourselves and others. We must strengthen and build up our own armories of resistance: independent institutions of governance, law, education, communication, information, transportation, and so on.

Furthermore, we must go into the conquered territories of our own society and seek out those who are courageous enough to join us. We must bring the invaluable munitions of skills and knowledge to our aid, encouraging the active participation of scientists, educators, analysts, writers, organizers, and technicians to leave the corporate-political regime and actively struggle for all of humankind.

Although I speak with military terms, I use such language only so that you will understand the ruthlessness of the war that is being waged against us. The corporate-political elite has bent the tools of civilization into the very swords with which they slaughter us. We must melt their swords back into ploughshares. The armories of civil society must be dismantled and reformed to our advantage. It can be done and this is how:

If our municipal corporations (known as city councils and county commissions) are being poised to uphold the domination of the corporate-political state, we should fearlessly use them as a bulwark against the onslaught of injustice even if it leads to the dissolving of the municipal body. In such cases, citizens must then, without hesitation or question, form a system of local self-governance, free from unjust laws or tyrannical destruction of life.

If our police officers are ordered to enforce the immoral, unconstitutional laws, then we must ask them to lay down their badges and stand with us as ordinary citizens. We must relieve them of duty if they comply with commands to use harmful and deadly force against those exercising their Constitutional Rights of Speech, Assembly, and Petition. If an entire police force is determined to maintain the power of corporate interests, then we must renounce their authority as illegitimate.

If our judicial system continues to repeat its long history of pandering to corporate interests to the detriment of the rights and well-being of the people, then we must ask our lawyers and judges to burn their licenses like draft cards, cast off the corrupted weight of precedence, and form arbitration courts such as those created by Gandhi and the Indian lawyers during the Self-Rule Movement.

If our academic institutions persevere in bending to corporate financial influence, then our young adults must leave the universities and colleges. Similarly, if our public education system continues to allow standardized testing to shape our precious children into obedient soldiers, unthinking consumers, and corporate loyalists, then we must remove our children and ask the teachers to walk out with us.

If our banks maintain the devastating trends of elitist favoritism, political domination, and enforcing the systems of wealth inequality, then we must withdraw our money down to the last penny. We must remove our investments in corporations of tyranny and destruction. We must pressure larger investors to relinquish the privilege of profit that comes at the price of human suffering.

This list is only partial. It must serve as a start to your own strategic thinking on this subject. These actions are not light, nor easy. The ramifications are profound. The Dandelion Insurrection wages struggle within and without the armories of our civilization. We do so nonviolently, but with strength and determination. When our social institutions fall into destructive hands, then we must challenge our courage to the extreme, release the corrupt and conquered halls of power, retreat to higher ground, and wage our struggle from a foundation of strength.

Throw Off the Yoke
of Indoctrination!

Essay Ten

We say we want change. So, every few years, we elect new officials, and they continue to churn out more of the same policies, legislation, and rhetoric. The rich continue to get richer. The poor slide deeper into poverty. Corporations and the wealthy get pet projects and sweet deals passed through Congress. The People receive yet another bitter slap in the face.

This is because the foundation of our nation is poisoned. The soil from which our people, elected officials, and politicians grow is toxic. Every generation is fed the same destructive falsehoods. By the time human beings become politicians they are massively propagandized to believe the purpose of public office is to make deals for big businesses … and from top to bottom we all continue to repeat the false slogan: *what's good for business is good for the nation.*

The wealthy and the corporations own the media, the entertainment industry, educational and cultural institutions, think tanks, research facilities, and, in short, every vehicle that defines our thoughts, beliefs, culture, perspectives and worldviews. They churn out mass propaganda that reinforces their power and control. And we ingest it, absorb it, and ultimately believe it.

Through this totalitarian control, the sicknesses that ail our country – lack of compassion, the valuing of profit and wealth above all else, justified cruelty, hatred and oppression – creep into the crevasses of our beliefs and worldviews, and take up toxic residence in our marrow. Layered and complex, this is the poisonous legacy of centuries of violence, conquest, bigotry, greed, supremacy, and domination. Many of us spew this garbage out of our words, thoughts, and actions . . . unless we consciously rebel against such mental indoctrination.

The path toward cultural and mental liberation is three-fold. We must first disconnect from the propaganda. We must unplug from corporate media: television, movies, books, entertainment, news, and magazines that are owned by the wealthy and promote - in subtle or blatant ways – the agendas of the wealthy. We must deny them access to our minds and fast from the programming that is otherwise pounded into our skulls on a daily basis.

Secondly, we must clear out the programming as it resurfaces in our minds. We must become aware of our thoughts and beliefs. We must learn to question them, critique them, dissect and analyze where they came from and whom they serve. Every craving for material goods must be examined to see if it originates in advertisements. Every inclination toward hatred, discrimination, or fear must be interrogated to see if it serves the desire of the wealthy to use us to oppress others, or to wage wars for their profits. Every thought that lauds the wealthy should be questioned deeply. From fairy tales to rags-to-riches stories to economic theories in business schools, we have absorbed their propaganda. Everything we think we know must be critiqued if wish to free our minds, and if we hope to see real change in our world.

Thirdly, we must rebuild the framework of our worldviews and perspectives. To truly rebel against the programming and propaganda of an oppressor is not merely to kick out their agenda, but to replace it with principles, beliefs, and understandings of our own.

However, if it is true liberation we seek, then a word of caution must be spoken here. Fleeing one form of mental slavery into dogmatic subservience to another is still enslaving your mind. Liberation is about freedom. It entails exploration, examination, reflection, openness, adaptability, and flexibility. The most truly radical and revolutionary people are the ones who dance through the tangled webs of perspectives and beliefs, engaging with ideas, but not clinging to them. These are the kinds of people that all tyrants fear. They are uncontrollable by others, yet responsible to their compassion and the demands of accountability set in place by the heart.

When such free thinkers become not lone individuals, but thousands and millions of citizens, empires tremble in their boots. Tyrants and bullies know their days are numbered. Pedagogues and warmongers fail to gain traction for their domination games.

If we wish to see deep, profound change in our politics, society, and culture, this is the mental liberation we must cultivate in our selves and our communities. Only then will our elected officials have the necessary freedom of thought to throw off the yoke of indoctrination. Only then will we ourselves have the capacity to form and shape our society in a way that cares for and nurtures everyone, not just a privileged few. Only then will we become truly free human beings, the kind of people we were always meant to be.

Rise and Resist

The United States
of Greed and Bullies

Essay Eleven

A nation built on greed is not a nation; it is merely a legal framework for rape and pillage, slavery and exploitation, theft, murder, and genocide. A nation whose primary function is to protect the exclusive right of the rich to engage in those behaviors under other names has no more moral legitimacy than the lawless state that allows common criminals to run wild. Greed by any other name smells just as foul. Greed cloaked in terms of "national security" or "for the good of the economy" is just as detestable as the greed that steals toys from children and purses from old women.

Greed is not a founding principle for a long-lasting society. It is the calling card of tyrants. It heralds the end stages of empires. It is the character flaw of villains. It is the symptom of sociopaths. The greed of the rich and powerful, particularly the corporate elites, has reached such magnitude that it outstrips our ability to describe it. We have no word for a theft so massive that it robs the ecological savings of eons, enslaves seven billion people to the machinery of profit-production, and steals the future existence of millions of species, including our own. It is genocide, ecocide, and slavery all rolled into one. It steals not just resources and lives, but thoughts,   dreams,   hopes,   happiness,   freedoms,   and

49

possibilities. All of these are chained to the production of profit for a small elite.

Every aspect of our human existence is mined for profit. Our thoughts. Our insecurities. Our longings. Our desires. Our sensuality and sexuality. Our health. Our sickness. Our fear, communications, visions, charity, and all other qualities. We are mined for any shred of human existence that could generate the smallest percentage of profit for the rich and powerful. They mine our personal histories. They mine our present data. They mine our future through debt.

Mine. Mine. Mine.

This greed has no name. There are no limits to its pathology. The economic system constructed by the unbridled greed of the elites trains us to replicate its values. It is like being held under water until we learn to fight for a single breath of air. Greed is not "normal" for humanity. We are not born with a hoarding instinct. If we were born with unbridled greed we would never stop sucking at our mother's breast until her entire lifeblood is drained into our engorged bellies. Greed is not an evolutionarily sound principle. Instead, something makes most infants stop at satiation point. That something makes us human. The greed of contemporary civilization is inhumane. It makes us into monsters.

We have a name for children who behave in this way: bullies. A bully invades another child's yard and takes all their toys. A bully patrols the playground forcing other children to pay lunchbox tolls to enter. A bully uses violence to get what they want. A bully terrorizes and intimidates to maintain their power and position. A bully refuses to share and play with others.

When bullies are lauded as the great leaders of a nation,

that nation has lost all worth. When bullies are celebrated as icons, that nation's culture has lost its soul. When bullies are empowered by law rather than constrained by law, that nation's legal system has become the tool of tyranny.

Our nation is a land of psychotic greed and bullies. It is up to us to change it. Every moment of every day, we must draw lines in the sand – the sand of the heart, the sand of our minds, the sand of our streets and workplaces. We must push back against the behaviors that this greed-and-bully culture has violently pounded into us. We must free ourselves from these mental chains, recognizing them as the enslavements that they are. We must call a spade, a spade. We must call a bully, a bully. We must reject our culture's hero worship of the rich and powerful. Instead, we must see these people for the depraved criminals that they are.

Behind every fortune are millions of hungry children. Behind every mansion are thousands of homeless people sleeping in the street. Behind every sports car are hundreds of families stretching to make ends meet. Behind every fancy party are the lost hopes and abandoned dreams of an entire populace.

Until we see excessive wealth as a cruelty when others cannot even survive, we will be a hollow nation, lacking any real meaning or worth. Until we love our country enough to care for it – each and every single citizen, tree, river, animal, and plant of it; the past, present, and future of it; the heart, spirit, and soul of it – until we love our country enough to topple greed from its enshrinement in our nation's policies and practices, we will never be able to lift our heads with honest pride. Until we stop our leaders from bullying and our bullies from becoming leaders, we will never become the nation that we are meant to be.

We will never be great. We will never be strong. We will never even be human until we have left the ways of greed and bullies behind.

Schoolyard Bullies on Capitol Hill

Essay Twelve

Politicians have devolved into nothing more than schoolyard bullies stealing lunch money from small children, harassing the defenseless, and expecting to receive gold stars of approval.

They plunder the public coffers, destroying shared wealth that we, the People, have worked arduously to build. With social justice movements, one after another, we have labored to defend these systems that protect and support our mothers, children, elders, families, the differently-abled, the down-on-their-luck, the hurt and abused. We have demonstrated our compassion for one another through insisting that our politicians institute these social programs. We have stood up for one another by defending them from the greedy plundering of bullies.

But politicians and their corporate, oligarchic cronies pervert media to their purposes and deceive the unsuspecting. They lie through their teeth to take lollipops from kindergarteners. They twist truth to get snacks from first graders. They strong-arm suspicious kids to get ahold of their goodies. They flat-out attack their peers to steal public lands, sweet deals of contracts, and the sustenance of subsidies.

If they don't get what they want, they throw tantrums. If they sense defiance, they beat it back into submission. If they get caught in the act, they turn on false charm to sway the authorities into letting them off with a wrist slap. If that doesn't work, they threaten to send in their big daddies of lawsuits, leverage, and clout.

These are the people running our country. We all know them – or at least, we've all encountered the grade school forerunners of this archetype. We've been slammed up against lockers, had gum stuck in our hair, been taunted and mocked, and tripped up in the halls of life.

We must deal with this problem of bullies occupying Capitol Hill. Bullies do not vanish by avoiding them . . . they simply go pick on someone else, grow bigger, and ultimately come back to haunt us from corporate offices and political seats. Wherever there is power, the abuse of power can exist. And inside each abuser is a bully that must be rousted.

It takes courage to stand up to bullies. They are strong and powerful. We feel weak and small. But, we are many and they are few . . . and when a whole schoolyard unites against tyranny and injustice, no bully can withstand our opposition.

We cannot use violence – it would turn us into the very monster we are seeking to transform. We must use noncooperation. We must refuse to be allies to bullies, pawns in his game, or part of his group. We must refuse to consent or comply to his demands. Neither fear nor ambition should sway us to give him what he wants to take through force. We must use collective protest: whenever and wherever we see a bully shaking down a first grader or snatching something from a kindergartener, we must collectively raise our voices and shout: *Stop! No more!* All eyes should turn on the bully. All voices must denounce the behavior.

We must courageously intervene, throwing our bodies over the defenseless, taking blows meant for another, and staring down hatred and violence. We must use de-escalation, distraction, and all the skills that can thwart a bully in his attempt to abuse others.

Together, we must lift up our shared values of kindness, compassion, and respect. We must treat one another as we wish to be treated. We must assert that these are the rules of our playground. We must insist that all who share our schoolyard and community play by the common rules of human decency. We must be willing to transform ourselves from isolated victims into collective movements for change.

And we must be willing to allow bullies to transform back into ordinary human beings. They are not monsters. They are humans. We must stand, as Dr. King said, against the injustice, yet not against the person. This may be the hardest task for us all. But at the end of the day, our schoolyard is part of our home, our community, and our nation. All of us – bullies, victims, scapegoats, bystanders, and defenders – will continue to live and work here. So, we must challenge and change the dynamics at play. We must end the bullying of others in our halls, seats, and offices of power. We must do so nonviolently with equal measures of courage and compassion. And we must strive to help everyone emerge from the gauntlet of change with our humanity intact, and our heads lifted high.

Rise and Resist

How to Fight a Tyrant

Essay Thirteen

It is not enough to hurl your rage at tyranny . . . every bully knows how to dodge a hothead. Anger is the alcohol of emotions. We flush, courageous in its drunken heat, but our blows miss, we flail, and our opponent easily dispatches us.

I've had my share of schoolyard skirmishes. I've been provoked and beaten soundly. I've swung my fist in honest rage . . . and missed. More times than I would like to count, my temper tripped me into fights. I won some; I lost others.

I've come to this: anger is a weakness.

Some claim it serves no purpose. "Righteous" anger is often lauded. Righteous or not, experience warns me that my anger has served me poorly - but my loss of control has aided my opponents greatly.

My days of playground scuffles are over, but the gang of bullies who now harass me are the greatest tyrants in the world. Their weaponry of authority, military, police, legalities, and money far outstrip the fistfights of my younger days. I cannot afford to take a swing and miss. Yes, I often feel my anger rising; their affronts are worse than when they made catcalls at my mother or whistled at my sweetheart; they're forcing my fellow men to slave for them, kicking children in the ribs, smacking women across the cheek, starving old ladies, forcing families out of homes, refusing healthcare to the sick – the causes of fury are real and just. Anger boils in me, volcano-like, but I will not let it erupt.

Tyrants easily endure eruptions. Fury falls as impotent as ash. Our opponents will simply flick it aside with self-satisfied smirks, order our people to clean up the broken glass and pools of blood on sidewalks, and continue on as if nothing happened.

No, I will not merely inconvenience them with my eruption. Anger is a force, more powerful when held in check. I'll convert it into determination, send its pressure underground, shake the foundations of their empire, and create hairline fractures in their fortresses. I will study the structures of their social skyscrapers, find their weaknesses, and erode the supporting pillars that allow tyranny to reign.

Channel your anger into determination for change. Become a force, unstoppable. Pull fury's heat deep down inside you. The blaze of anger's fire can blind you; its smoke obscures the mind. Become a master smith of your emotions. Red flames cannot bend iron . . . but white-hot coals melt steel. This is the intensity that is required to fight these tyrants. Stark clarity of mind provides power to our actions. The rational mind is our weapon – never let it go! Only a fool would fling it aside and leap at a tyrant with bare fists.

You are no fool, and neither am I. Nor can we call our opponents such. Callous they may be, greedy, cruel, but let no one call them fools. They are sharp, educated, intelligent, cunning, but I will tell you a secret . . . the tyrant's intelligence can count up people; but only wisdom explains what moves them. Brains can order brawn around; but only wisdom reveals what makes people refuse to follow orders. Any tyrant can send soldiers into battle; but wisdom can convince them to lay down their guns.

Intelligence never conquers wisdom . . . and at this we shall excel.

Rise and Resist

The Three Thefts

When the forces of destruction, hate, bigotry, greed, and violence rise into power, there are three things they steal before they plunder the treasury. Stopping them is where the struggle for life begins.

The first thing they steal is courage. The forces of destruction must snuff out the courage of the people like a candle in a harsh autumn wind. Fear must pervade the nooks and crannies of the heart and mind. Frightened shivers must weaken the spines of the people. It is easy to conquer people who scurry out of danger or hide from fear.

The second theft is hope. To achieve the goals of greed and hatred, the people must be bogged down in the morass of hopelessness and despair. So, they steal our hope, bound and gagged like Demeter's daughter, and shove it into the underworld of impossibility while the cold winter of hopelessness freezes us in its grip.

The third thing they steal is joy. Sly and clever, they ferret out the small things in which the human heart delights and one-by-one, they rob us of our joy. Where they cannot take the physical sources of our happiness, they sneakily insinuate guilt . . . making us feel guilty for feeling joy in the midst of the world's madness.

Joy is the place where our resistance must draw a line in the sand and begin to push back. Your joy is a wild and beautiful thing. In the midst of insanity, destruction, violence, greed, it is a force of strength and liberation, love and hope. The leaves falling in autumn, the breathless hush of snow, a cup of tea, a slice of bread, the company of a good friend, the smiles of children, the eyes of someone you love . . . to feel joy in these beauties is a powerful resistance to the tide of destruction. It is the ground of existence and the source of strength for resistance. Draw a line here. Let your joy defy the forces of hate and despair. Lift up your joy as the motivation to meet hated with love; destruction with creation; greed with generosity; and violence with active, powerful nonviolence.

When your hopes are dashed, bound, gagged, silenced and mocked, go – like Persephone's mother – into the underworld of despair and rescue them. Bring them back to life like the first buds on the branches in spring. Withstand the hot-cold crosswinds of change, and dare to lift your hopes aloft for everyone to see. If they are knocked down, pick them up. If they are trivialized, resist. Where there is hope, there is life. A world without hope is a world locked in the darkness that cannot remember the dawn. This is nonsense. Every two-day-old baby knows that sunrise is coming. Every child has seen how spring returns after winter. Hope is woven into our existence. It is our treasure. Don't allow it to be kidnapped from your heart.

As for courage, this is the most important of all. When fear lands on your shoulders like a hunchbacked demon, gripping your neck in the twisted clench of its fingers, suffocating your chest, clouding your eyes . . . fight back. Fling it off, again and again. Wrestle with fear until you break free. The heat of that struggle is called courage – the fire in your veins, the flush of life in your muscles, the breath in your chest, the pounding of your heart as you break free of the clutches of fear.

There is more, too, that we can do in the ground of resistance. We can cultivate clarity, centeredness, and presence. When we lose these qualities, it is easy for us to be thrown off-balance, shoved to the side, pushed down, confused, and defeated. The forces of hate, destruction, violence, and greed are all delighted when we allow our minds to become scattered and ungrounded. We become easy to fight, to trample, and to destroy. So, our resistance must cultivate clarity and focus to give us strength and capacity to wage struggle.

There are also other treasures of the human heart that the forces of destruction try to steal or weaken: love, a sense of injustice, rebelliousness, stubbornness. But, these are tenacious capacities of the human heart. It takes the forces of destruction longer to chisel them out of us. We must draw the line at the three treasures of courage, hope, and joy. With them, we can stand firm in the madness. We can shine light in the darkness of destruction. We can draw upon the wellspring of strength that has nurtured humanity through eons of time. We can enter the struggle prepared with courage, joy, hope, clarity, vision, connection, and love. With these strengths we will succeed.

Rise and Resist

Fling Back Despair!
Kindle the Flame of Hope!

Essay Fifteen

Despair rides in front of our opposition, an invisible wind that blows like plague through our hearts. Here, our stand begins. Moment-by-moment, day-by-day, we must keep despair at bay in the siege waged by the forces of destruction and greed.

I have written about the three treasures – courage, hope, and joy – and how the foes of life and love seek to steal or destroy them. Guard the three treasures well. Thieves come in the guises of both friends and enemies. Without courage, hope, and joy, despair can crumble the strongest to their feet. It can cripple the smartest minds. It can weaken the boldest hearts. It spreads, infectious, from one person to the next, until the whole populace sinks to its knees, and the armies of greed and destruction trample over us.

Here is how to thwart despair and deny this invisible fiend any toehold in your heart: first, collect stories of the good, the kind, the loving, and the hopeful. Gather them in the storehouse of your mind. When despair begins to sneak in, hold up these stories to push back. Remember the examples of successes and victories. Think about people who made change when it all seemed impossible. Invoke the characters both historic and living that continue to inspire you in your own life. Borrow strength from the tangible, honest stories of sheer goodness: people who care for the weak, the laughter of children, the taste of a humble bowl of soup. Collect gentle balms like the blossoms of flowers, the sound of a stream, the swoop of a bird's flight, the sunlight dancing through trees. Hold all of these in your heart for the times when you need the reminder that life is worth the challenges we face.

And, in those times when the smothering fog of despair dampens the kindled flame of hope, then we must sing out with love in the midst of the darkness. If the shape of our love begins in sorrow, so be it, let it flow out, and reach deeper. Beneath the sadness is usually something extraordinary: a powerful love for each other and this earth. Sometimes, the song of our love comes out in quiet presence, a simple hum of existence, a reassurance that we are here and alive in one another. Other times, our love sings in a fierce determination, a resurrection song that refuses to give up. Sing out your love in whatever its shape, so that others may hear and lift up their voices with yours. Dare to love this world and each other in all of our uncertainty, all of our brokenness, and all of our humanness. Where love stands, despair retreats. In that space, we find the strength to move forward.

We can also raise up the vision of the world we seek, even when despair howls that it will never come to be. We must lift up that vision, blazing, in the dark night. We must dare to believe in the world that we envision, to speak of it, share it with others, and remind one another of its beauty. This takes courage, but it is courage well spent, for a single torch of vision can illuminate the ground beneath our feet. And when you touch the flame of your vision to the extinguished torch of a friend, and she to her neighbor, and he to his companion, and so on – until we are all standing as a thousand, ten thousand, one million points of light – then the entire slope of the mountain gleams. The path emerges beneath us. Despair is flung back. We rise and move forward, up to the mountaintop. And the dawn of change greets us, brighter than a billion torches of hope, rising over the very world we dared to dream of when the night seemed too dark, and the slope seemed too steep, and despair weighed on us too heavy to bear.

So, do this work, my friends. Fortify your hearts. Build up your ability to thwart despair. See it as yet another assault from the forces of destruction, and refuse to surrender so easily to them. Train in these practices. Apply them as despair creeps closer. Teach them to others. Together, we will light up the mountainside and climb onward to the world we envision.

Rise and Resist

Corporate Demons
Possess Our Nation's Soul

Essay Sixteen

Corporate demons possess our nation's soul. They crept in stealthily, full of trickery and deception, but now they're lodged in place, as surely as if they had stormed our homes and halls of power with guns and tanks. Perhaps we'd recognize their coup if they had assassinated a flesh-and-blood president instead of merely stealing the souls of all our elected leaders.

A corporation is an invisible entity. It has no body to appear on television or slip into a congressional seat. It works by proxy, roping in living, breathing human worshippers to kill, maim, and destroy for the sake of its corporate greed. For a lump of money, a human soul is bought and turned into the pawn of corporations. For a bribe or a salary, a human being averts their eyes and does the dirty work. For a sweet deal, a real-life person decides to allow a corporation to injure and oppress, impoverish and harm.

Without us, corporations are nothing more than words written on documents. They cannot drill for oil. They cannot foreclose on homes. They cannot deliver eviction notices. They cannot pass legislation. They cannot poison water or spew toxins in the air. They cannot arrest those who rise up against them.

There are millions of people railing against corporate power in our government, and rightly so, for corporations have stolen the souls of public office holders. They have corrupted the hearts of elected leaders. They have bought the obedience of senators and representatives, judges and sheriffs and presidents. But the struggle is far vaster than just our political power-holders. It is not just a monetized, secularized, or politicized conflict. This struggle goes straight to the heart and soul of every man, woman, and child in this country.

Who is willing to be the first to evict corporate power from their heart? Among the citizens, who will expel the twin demons of our habit-forming consumer conveniences and corporate greed from our lives and pocketbooks. Who will decolonize their minds from the entertainment, advertisements, logos, slogans, and ideologies of the corporations? Who will refuse to bring one more purchase of the corporate overlords into his or her house? When the early American colonists were rebelling against the British, they sacrificed the luxuries of imported British cloth, tea, and more. Young girls wore dresses of homespun cloth to the old-fashioned versions of the prom. Among modern Americans, who is willing to sacrifice our ease, convenience, and consumerism in favor of freedom from political injustice?

If we want to evict corporations from Capitol Hill, we are going to have to evict them from our own lives in ways that will not be easy. We will have to sacrifice. We will have to make do and do without. We will have to pay more for the product from a local, small, or independent company that does not have the same economic advantages as mega-corporations who enjoy tax breaks and subsidies, the ability to pay unjust wages unchallenged, the luxury of externalizing the true costs of their products, the insider industry deals on shipping and bulk product purchasing, and much more.

But each time your heart balks at a sacrifice, look at the horizon of possibilities. Fix your eyes on the vision of what we're working toward . . . it is far greater than the sacrifices we face. We are striving toward functional democracy that represents, cares for, nurtures and sustains the whole of the populace, not just the ruling elite and corporate profit. We are working toward economic justice and vibrant, diverse, local, small, and independent businesses that have a fair and level playing field. We are moving toward the protection of the beautiful planet that keeps us all alive, renewable energy, and a world free of pollution and toxicity. We want political justice so that we can assure and maintain economic, cultural, racial, gender, and all other forms of justice. We want arts, culture, and entertainment driven not by monopoly and narrow agendas, but by the beauty and bounty of our diversity and many perspectives. The list goes on.

The possibilities on the horizon line of change are tremendous. Fix your eyes on them as we make changes in our own lives during the effort to erode and evict corporate power and greed. Remember what we're sacrificing for as we overthrow corporations from the halls of power of our country. We are struggling for the heart and soul of our nation. It is worth wrestling with the corporate demons until every last man, woman, and child is free.

Rise and Resist

Swine, Swill, and Silver Platters

Essay Seventeen

We are serving ourselves up on silver platters to the oligarchs and giant corporations. We have apples of misinformation in our mouths and sprigs of patriotic parsley tucked behind our ears. Must we complacently acquiesce to being pot-roasted pigs? Rise up!

The situation is more than intolerable - it is ridiculous; it is obscene. Our citizenry behaves like swine in the feedlots of the giant corporations and their rich owners. We eat the swill they slop down of toxic food, poisonous lies, mind-numbing media, and soul-crushing policies of oppression. We roll in the muck, too moribund to rise up and organize for life, liberty, and love!

Have you ever seen a wild boar? Hairy, black, powerful, untamed, muscular? Have ever seen the wild sow? Alert, protective, and nurturing of her young? Have you seen the natural liveliness and intelligence of the lithe, quick piglets raised in woodlands and meadows, not muck and feedlots?

Are you content to live out your days, numbed and enslaved, slated for the slaughterhouse? To be destined only to put profits into rich people's pockets? To be basted in lies and roasted in the fire of injustice? To be carved up slice-by-slice and devoured by gluttons? To condemn your children to the same fate?

Before there were masters and owners, overseers and

butchers, merchants and chefs, the pig was wild, untamed, and free. It chose where it roamed. It ate when hungry. It rested when tired.

It is said that the pig is more intelligent than the dog. Yet, most of its species is enslaved to the greed of human cravings. The human being is allegedly far more intelligent than the swine, and yet, under the surface of our acculturation, are we not locked in feedlots of work, rent, bills, and debt? Are not our whole lives one long production line for rich people's profits? Is not our freedom as equally illusory as the pig's, lasting only as long as no one attempts to break free?

These are unsettling questions. But when abattoirs and silver platters await us, perhaps we ought to be uneasy. Perhaps we ought to be eyeing the holes in the fences. Perhaps we ought to be discussing what would happen if we all refused to go quietly to the slaughterhouse. Perhaps we ought to stop eating the swill and let the pinch of hunger sharpen our eyes to the truth.

Impossible Courage

Wishful thinking and random action will not topple the corrupt and powerful collusion of extreme capitalism, the wealthy elite, and military force. For all the courage shown thus far by people across the country in demonstrating, petitioning, even throwing their bodies in the line of danger, I call upon an even greater courage now ...

... the courage to act like we stand a chance of winning.

Desperate acts of valor in the midst of despair, futile symbolic gestures, spontaneous eruptions of anger and violence: none of these require the same courage as sitting down and systematically analyzing how a tiny group of disorganized, overwhelmed, exhausted, contentious, and geographically dispersed people can bring about the downfall of a massive machine of economics, legislation, cultural brainwashing, media domination, law enforcement, surveillance, and military power.

That, my friends, requires the courage to confront the impossible.

It requires that we look unflinchingly at the horrors of this machine. It demands that we examine – and overcome – our own shortcomings. It also requires that we exhibit the bravery of the inventor, one who looks at the impossible and decides it can - and will – be done. The only question is: how?

Thomas Edison famously said, "Genius is one percent

75

inspiration and ninety-nine per cent perspiration. Accordingly, a 'genius' is often merely a talented person who has done all of his or her homework."

Inventors possess a great deal of two common human traits: curiosity and persistence. With these, they have flown like birds, split the atom, and landed on the moon – all impossible tasks that have been made possible by the determination to ask the right questions and seek the answers. Libraries have been written about the strategies of waging nonviolent struggle, but the central questions boil down to this:

- What are our strengths?
- What are our opponents' weaknesses?
- How can we wisely use our strengths to aggravate their weaknesses?

Dare to have the courage to pursue this line of questioning into the gritty details of the complicated picture that arises. Along the way, we might also ask:

- What are our weaknesses?
- What are our opponents' strengths?
- How can we lessen or eliminate our weaknesses while eroding the strengths of our opponents?

It is cowardice to balk from answering these questions. It is an act of denial and despair to engage in nonviolent struggle without tackling the analysis of strategy. It is ineffectual at best; sheer suicide at worst. Because, be assured, you are not alone in asking these questions. The corporations, the government, and the military all employ full-time staff to ask these questions about us.

At this moment in history, it is clear that reform of single issues will not resolve the dire nature of our situation. We must be bold enough to confront the entire collusion of wealthy elite, corporate politics, and military might. We must be determined to follow our questions into uncertain avenues and research the daunting forces that confront us. We must, in the words of Che Guevara, "Be realistic; demand the impossible!"

Our very lives – and all of earth – may depend on it.

Rise and Resist

Three R's They Don't Teach In School

Essay Nineteen

Resistance, rabble-rousing, rebellion: a maturing empire such as ours has no room for these. Unquestioning obedience is required. Every standardized test, multiple choice question, regimented schedule, gold star, or failing grade trains us to obey authority. The curriculum that is laid out in yearly tests leaves no time for free thought, only a frantic rush to memorize and regurgitate the correct answer.

It is boot camp for our brains.

From our leaders' viewpoint, American society no longer requires pioneers, artists, and innovators. The wealthy elite births just enough entrepreneurs to generate fresh, controllable income. Inventors are cheaper in China, where such questioning minds pose problems to other corrupt governments, not ours. Puppet artists who uphold the entrenched snobbery of the classical arts can be imported along with fine furniture and fancy electronics.

Our nation requires soldiers and servants – though impoverished citizens enslaved by debt will suffice if the correct attitudes of patriotism and servility cannot be inspired. It is best, however, if obedience can be drilled into the children from an early age. A questioning mind is a dangerous weapon. A dissenter could cause massive societal destruction. A dreamer who paints the world outside the corporate box is an undeniable enemy of the State.

The surly child slouching in the back row, drumming impatiently on his desk should be hauled up to the front of the class. Mock him! Shame him into line. Slap him with a ruler if you must! His rebellious soul should be imprisoned immediately.

That child must never be left to wander the library. He should never lay his hands on the stories of rebel-souls like Gandhi or Dr. King. He'll get dangerous ideas. He'll think that his disobedience has deep and noble roots. He should never hear the truth about the upstarts that ignited the American Revolution. Let him imagine that patriotism for America inspired those early radicals. Train him to love his country, to fight for it, to die for it! Hide the truth from that child. Don't point out that the yearning for freedom and independence from oppressive control preceded loyalty to one's country. Patriotism for America was a whiplash of control that cracked across our forefathers' backs. Don't tell that rule-breaking child about that.

The American Empire fears this child; he contains the seed of the Dandelion Insurrection. His soul knows the meaning of tyranny. His eyes recognize the signs of oppression. His mind fights the constraints of society. His heart is not afraid to risk everything to champion the rights of all. They will try to crush him, smash the seed of rebellion inside him, and bury the threat of his unruliness under the concrete of their control. They will teach the other children to hate and scorn him.

But adversity is the fertilizer of a true rebel. The seed inside that child will thrive against all odds.

I was that child, my friends, and if I could speak with him

now, I would give him courage for his arduous years. I would light the flame of hope inside him. I would assure him that the seed he carried in his soul would never die. He would see it, one day, lying dormant in all the other children. He would find it germinating in every man. He would see it curling in the women's hearts. And, one great morning, he will look at his country – as I do now – and see the seeds of the Dandelion Insurrection blossoming.

Rise and Resist

The Rule of the Rich
and the Last Hurrah

Essay Twenty

Rich people rule, make no mistake. They have ruled for centuries, and the toll of their reign has been high. At their feet can be laid the bodies of every child starved in a world with surplus food; every person who freezes to death in the streets while houses sit empty; every death from lack of affordable healthcare; and the incalculable casualties of the world's wars – which have all had the wealthy at the helm. Colonization's genocides, slavery's murders, and the living death of mass incarceration can all be added to the oligarchy's tally.

Most damning, we can now add the looming threat of mass extinction to the track record of the rich – for they are the ones who obscured climate science, who promoted denialism to protect fossil fuel profits, and who still obstruct the necessary transition to sustainable practices. Make no mistake: the rule of the rich has been a deadly epoch for humanity.

We cannot compare the effect of the rule of a whole populace empowered by democracy. In this country, the wealthy hijacked the idea of democracy starting in 1787 when the Constitution excluded everyone but propertied white males. There are few examples of full-constituency, class-balanced democracy throughout human history. In no case can the scale of destruction be compared to what the rule of the rich has done.

We owe them no allegiance. They have shown their reign to be dangerous, deadly, and destructive. We owe it to ourselves, our communities, humanity, and the Earth to utterly resist their continued rule. We must reject their propaganda. We must recognize it on billboards and movie screens. We must learn to see how it masquerades in education and spouts from the mouths of politicians. Every sector of our lives currently serves to prop up the rule of the rich, their ideologies and worldviews. Effective resistance begins by silencing our cheers and breaking our silence when the next dose of propaganda is being spoon-fed to the nation.

It is not a matter of "good" billionaires vs. "bad" billionaires. Like benevolent dictators, the system itself is rotten to the core. It will never represent the needs of the people. There are no safeguards against tyrants. Those who cheer on their favorite gladiator of a billionaire are deluding themselves about the nature of power and wealth. Billionaires can turn the sharp sword's edge of their power against you. Their economic empires will subjugate you for profit. It is foolish to applaud philanthropy without examining the sources of the fortune. Do not let the rain of money blind you. Beneath the glamour lies a complex equation that nets a savings for your favorite wealthy darling of a donor, privatizing the use of money while robbing it from any hope of democratic application that taxation might have offered. Those fortunes showered on charities and foundation grants have been skimmed from wages, market manipulation, high-priced products, and often government subsidies.

There are no "good" plutocrats, not when you look closely. You can have democracy or you can have the rule of the rich. You cannot have both. On their side, the rich offer a hedonistic last hurrah, an orgy of plundering and partying for a brief firework-explosion of a moment before the unending eternity of extinction. On our side, we lift the glimmer of hope, the tendril-seed chance of life.

You choose.

Rise and Resist

Send Me Your Blessings, Oh Angels of People!

Essay Twenty-One

There is a despair that grips the heart as I watch them fall around me: the too-thin young mother looking for work; the pain-ridden woman with no healthcare; the husband without answers to his wife's worried questions; the preacher who weeps as he prays for God's help; the youth sentenced harshly in a mockery of justice; the faces swollen from the beatings of cops . . .

My life is a bullet shot at the heart of their suffering.

Other people are angels, sent down to soothe, to assuage constant hunger, to keep off the chill, to provide houses for children, hope for the parents . . . but I have been fired from the cannon of justice and am hurtling full speed toward change. I have emptied my pockets to speed up my flight. My coins have fed children. My coat warms another. I spent my kind words as fast as I found them. Now, emptied and lightened, my whole self races faster, but despair is the wind that resists me.

It is hard to watch people cry out and not soothe them – it hurts to keep hurtling forward this way – but the thousands of soup kitchens, shelters, and charities are but Band-Aids without the arc of this flight.

Don't resent me, oh angels, because I race past. Send me

your blessings, instead. Point out my flight to the child you comfort. Tell them I'm heading to the root of their suffering and love is the force that propels me. Tell them I hear them, see them, and care. I'm not passing by without noticing their tears. I can't feed them today, nor house them tonight. I can't lift off their worries, or take away sorrows . . . but my life is a single-shot bullet that streams to the heart of the causes of their suffering.

Tell them, oh angels, so they don't misunderstand me. It is easy to love people who alleviate symptoms, but harder to love doctors who must speak the raw truth. Pain will not vanish without massive change. Hunger will continue, unchecked. If we don't work hard at politics, we will work hard in poverty. Healthcare won't fall from the sky. Justice is not made by rich judges in robes; justice is wrought by the people. Struggle lies before us – change never comes easily – but our other option is to lie down and die.

Our suffering is legion, our problems many; the causes abound and proliferate . . . but these conditions originate in cold, closed up hearts – human hearts that control, horde, and withhold; humans that write policies of greed; humans who order war, violence, and beatings as if they were dishes from the menu of hatred; humans with blind eyes, deaf ears, and stubborn minds; humans who have closed off their hearts.

My life is a bullet shot toward them all, but my impact will not bring them death . . . for love is the force that propels me. Love rips through their policies, tears up the rulebooks, kicks out corruption, and truncates their greed.

So, send me your blessings, oh angels of people, for this is the change that I bring!

Not One Penny More to the Rich

Essay Twenty-Two

When times are bleak and darkness deepens, ancient yearnings of humanity stir in our hearts. We long for the simple things that our ancestors always sought: safety for our families, roofs over our heads, food in our bellies, rest for our weary bodies. In other words, we yearn for the basic human rights that have been denied to far too many generations over the course of human history.

Throughout large swaths of history, the average human has been strapped to the yoke of economic injustice. Today, we are chained to jobs and bills and mounting debt. We are the workhorses of the modern-day wealthy. We labor to build their massive fortunes in a repetition of history as old as slaves building the pyramids, conscripts constructing the Great Wall of China, or the peons and peasants laboring to build the castles and cathedrals of Europe.

Today, we raise skyscrapers instead of temples, mansions instead of palaces, and astronomical off-shore bank accounts instead of treasure troves; but the pattern is the same. The wealth that could support the well-being of a whole society is hoarded by the few. And worse than hoarded: it is stolen, skimmed, raked off the backs of many. It is snatched from our lives in slivers and slices. They take pennies and dollars from millions of us to make themselves rich: a high utility bill, an increase in the rent, overdraft fees at the banks, a new replacement cord for the computer – small things, multiplied by millions, collected by a few; tiny percentages of pennies that add up to our impoverishment. Even the least significant laws and policies – which are written by the wealthy – affect the rich and poor disproportionately. To those with money, a hundred-dollar parking ticket is an inconvenience. To those without wealth, it might be the straw upon the camel's back, the calamity that leads to eviction or homelessness, or the shortfall that signals hunger for one's kids.

The rich grow richer while the rest of society suffers. They demand that walls be built to protect their fortunes – large or small – from those who have had everything taken from them in the cycles of injustice. Such hoarding of wealth while others are in need is obscene. It has been since the age of cavemen and campfires. It was appalling when the feudal kingdoms arose around the world. It was shameful when hierarchies of rulers emerged and feasted while their so-called subjects hungered. It is wrong, now, that the wealthy fly around the world in private jets while ordinary people struggle to pay bills.

Longevity does not lessen the shame of the injustice. It burns as fresh and hot in the thousandth year of its existence as it did on the first day a child went hungry because a glutton ate her share of the family's food. The complexities of global economics fall away before the simplicity of compassion. Humanity's soul remains imperiled when some hoard while others hunger.

And who dares to demand the impossible? Who is bold enough to speak the moral truth?

Not one penny more should go to the rich until every human being has enough. Not one more dollar should be added to the stockpiles of the wealthy while anyone is hungry, homeless, sick, or indebted due to seeking education, health, or survival. We must draw the moral line in the sand of our thoughts. We must cease the attitudes of permissibility that allow the greedy to hoard with such impunity. We must be clear and firm about our values. We must declare that enough is truly enough.

Rise and Resist

Throw Off the Tyranny of Poverty!

Essay Twenty-Three

Curse the war culture! It leaves us at a loss for words, bereft of metaphors to describe our situation. Our minds become blank slates, unable to recognize dangers at the door unless they carry assault weapons or drop bombs on our heads.

Studies have shown that poverty will kill more of us than terrorism – one hundred people die each hour from poverty and poverty-related social factors. And yet, our politicians scrounge up terrorist bogeymen to scare us! If we wanted to find a heart-chilling monster, we could simply look at the bloodsucking greed that impoverishes us and cripples us with unending debt.

What more do we need to rise into action? Do we need bombs instead of bank policies to make this crisis clear? Do we need soldiers with bayonets pounding down our doors instead of lawyers and bill collectors in suits and ties? There is nothing metaphorical about a danger that robs the breath from 2,400 citizens each day! There is no excuse for the political inaction that fails to protect and defend the hundreds of thousands who will die from poverty and poverty-related social factors each year!

Mobilize! Gather the hot-blooded and cool-headed in your community. Drill and train in nonviolent action with all the ferocity of traditional boot camp. Turn out the ranks – young and old – of people who can wield a boycott, build a blockade, charge in with a divestment campaign, sound the clarion call to march and protest, and more.

With the tools of nonviolent action in our hands, we become a powerful force. Strikes, shutdowns, walkouts, noncooperation, civil disobedience, and more: these tools are twice as effective as violent means at overthrowing tyrannical regimes, repelling foreign invasions, and ending occupations. And what is poverty, but an occupying power that dictates cruel edicts that cause suffering and oppression in our lives?

Poverty cannot be stopped by bullets, but it can be halted, pushed back, and sent running by organized nonviolent action. We can challenge and transform the systemic underlying causes of concentrated wealth, lack of real democracy, oligarchic rule, corporate greed, unjust laws, the shackles of debt practices, lack of economic justice, and the corruption of cultural values that give rise to the permissibility of hoarding, greed, plundering, looting, and stealing. We can wage nonviolent struggle against each of these on every level from national politics to massive corporate policies to local businesses and the hidden workings of the human heart.

We need not wait for bombs or bullets to see clearly where the danger lies. Today, thousands of people will die waiting for us to mobilize and succeed. Tomorrow, thousands more will die if we do not rally to stop the danger pounding on our doors. Day in and day out, the casualties mount while we flounder. Those who feel the tightening stranglehold of poverty crushing the life breath from their chests are crying out. The tools of change are at hand! Wake up! Seize the day, organize, train, resist, and build to chase the tyranny of poverty away.

Overthrow the Corporate Overlords

Essay Twenty-Four

If you like being a peon, a serf, or a slave, by all means, continue on with business-as-usual. Your corporate overlords are delighted to exploit you. They're thrilled at the prospect of profiting off your descendants for all eternity. But their hourglass is running out of sand. The planet's ecosystems are collapsing. We will not last long as underlings. This is a paltry comfort as we slide toward mass extinction.

If your heart rebels against this fate, you must stir yourself to action. You must weigh the peril of our looming future against the dangers of resistance. Your fear of repression from the familiar tyrants must be measured against the potential threats coming from forest fires, floods, hurricanes, droughts, famines, and mass poverty. As bad as it is, it can get worse. And it will. To resist is to live. To believe in life and to cherish humanity is survival.

The problem is that many of us have become comfortable with the status quo. The brutalities of the present are as familiar as an abusive partner. Leaving them takes more than courage. It takes vision for a better future.

We must dare to ask – and answer – the question: who and what will replace the corporate overlords?

The answer is a long-cherished dream of humanity, a once robust vision of self-governance and real democracy. History is written by the conquerors, and the dominators' history books obscure the truth that we used to govern ourselves. From kings to nobles to plutocrats to corporate overlords, those who pillage, plunder, oppress, and enslave have rewritten the story of humanity. They claim we must be ruled by a wise (and hopefully benevolent) overlord. This is a lie. Once upon a time, in a history forgotten to contemporary humans, we made our decisions together. Archeology points to a time before conquest and violence. It shows graves of egalitarian wealth, no man or woman richer or more noble than the rest. It tells of a time before patriarchy and war. The history books rarely mention this . . . or any other real democratic and shared decision-making systems throughout the centuries. The dominators' history will wax poetic about kings and emperors, warlords and nobles. It will leave out the history of the Norse "Things", the randomly-selected government positions of Greece, the Commons of Europe, the consensus-based organizing of movement groups, the longevity of numerous anarchist collectives, and the tribal democracies of the Iroquois, Wabanaki, and others.

We need to know these stories. They are the complex and varied answers to our question of what comes after the revolution. We know it will not be – cannot be – more of the same. The current systems of elitist power have squandered their legitimacy to rule, especially corporate power. From the first charters of companies like the East India, they have enslaved, massacred, destroyed, exploited, extracted, starved, impoverished, overthrown, oppressed, poisoned, robbed, humiliated, and murdered anything that stood between them and their greed.

Continuing to tolerate them is a death sentence. Resisting them with organized nonviolent struggle is the most courageous and sensible response. The full arsenal of nonviolence must be deployed: we must build robust alternatives to corporatism and capitalist-consumer culture, organize widespread participation in alternative economies like gifting, sharing, commoning, trade and barter, time banks, local currencies, and more. We must wrest the state apparatus out of the hands of oligarchs and corporatists using electoral, legislative, and direct action. We must pick away at the structural and systemic injustices that keep elites in power, including problems like voter disenfranchisement, money as speech, the two-party duopoly, gerrymandering, and more.

We must use coordinated strikes and boycotts in the economic sector to limit the power of corporations over people and planet. We must support and join cooperatives, democratizing the means of production. We must make corporations accountable to citizens and citizen legislative bodies. Local communities must be able to halt the poisoning of the land, water, air, and people.

We cannot sustain this predicament of corporate overlords and serfs. It is rebel or die. I know what I choose. Do you?

Rise and Resist

What Are We Waiting For?

Essay Twenty-Five

We wait . . . we wait for another scandal to validate our suspicions of corruption . . . as if the abuse of power is not enough to demand impeachment and reform.

We wait for a courageous Thomas Jefferson to declare our independence . . . as if we did not already know the long list of grievances that should ignite our second revolution.

We wait for the outbreak of millions of people rioting in the streets . . . as if we need a mob to find the courage to rebel against tyranny.

Reform, revolution, rebellion; regardless of what we yearn for, we wait. The straws pile high on the camel's back; we wait. The injustices mount; we wait. The freedoms of our nation crumble; we wait.

For what?

Do we seek some further proof that our cause is just? Do we need one more slap in the face? Or another blatant abuse of privilege by the wealthy? Or the next devastating environmental disaster?

No. What we await is the readiness of the people. We look around and at ourselves and see that the populace is unprepared. We are sleepy, sick, reactionary, violent, uneducated, unaware, apathetic, and frightened. This is not encouraging material for waging struggle.

So, frustrated and uncertain, we wait. But, by the time an

affront insulting enough slaps the populace awake, it will be too late. Our opponents will be readied and amassed on our doorsteps while we struggle to pull on our pants and stumble out of bed. By the time the next disaster strikes, it will be too late to take the wreck of our populace and rally them to sensible action.

My friends, I applaud your passion and your courage, but the military commanders of our opponents are laughing at us. They know that civilians cannot be snatched off the street and thrust immediately into battle – not if the commanders intend to win a war. Yet, the Dandelion Insurrection seems to think we can sound the trumpet and our nonviolent army will come pouring into the streets.

If we do not mobilize our people and train them in nonviolent struggle as thoroughly as the military builds their forces of violent warfare, then we will be slaughtered whenever and wherever we take a stand against the corporate-political state. We will watch, impotent, as they destroy all that we love.

And so, I urge us neither to act without preparation, nor to wait, but instead to build our forces in three ways:

Reform, which entails overhauling yourselves, your friends, families, and communities, your inner awareness, physical health; and preparing mentally and emotionally for the struggle we face.

Revolution, which requires thinking carefully about the problems of the current system, proposing radical solutions, and creating a new society, leaving no stone unturned in the complete re-visioning of government, education, economy, and social institutions.

Rebellion, through organizing and training in nonviolent

strategy, methods, and philosophy – which is the most effective act of rebellion you can commit at this time. Think of yourself as David slinging practice stones. Goliath did not fall to an untrained child. He fell to a young man of skill and strategy – a young man compelled to action by a sense of injustice – a young man prepared to fight a tyrant.

The metaphor of David and Goliath does not stop there. Ends are the means in the making; the manner in which we wage struggle becomes the world we will end up in. David was an underdog-turned-victor who murdered a bully and then went on to a lifetime of butchery and conquest, claiming God as his justification, and unleashing centuries of persecution and warfare that continue to this day.

The time of the Old Testament has long since passed. Our Goliath is a many-headed monster armed with drones and nuclear bombs, but we now wield a force far more powerful than slingshots. Jesus has walked this earth, and Gandhi, King, Chavez, and countless more. They brought us nonviolent struggle, which has become the tool of all humanity in working for change. We will be saved not by a chosen one, but by us all.

So, hold off on taking potshots at Goliath. Prepare for struggle en masse. Never has there been an underdog more unlikely than we. Never has there been an opponent more fearsome than this corporate-political empire. Never has the cause been more precious: this earth and all her children – including ourselves, our little ones, and the future of humanity.

Rise and Resist

Censorship:
the Death Knell of Democracy

Essay Twenty-Six

Censorship is the foe of freedom. It comes in many forms. The choking grip of control silences dissent. The bullhorns of propaganda blare out lies and fictions of consent. The maddened clench of greed stifles outlets for a diversity of expression, creativity, opportunity, and invention. The lurking spies of mass surveillance send chills down once-fearless spines. The data collectors of corporations mine our lives for ways to shrink-wrap our world views into commoditized sales pitches.

We think of censorship as cutting off a voice or silencing an outspoken dissenter. It is much worse . . . censorship today happens at every level of society from our minds to our platforms to our search engines. We dream in tight little boxes of permissible ideas. We speak only what others wish to hear. We gain access to platforms only by conforming to comfortable lies. If an uncomfortable truth manages to leap the hurtles and reach the outer rim of a listener's ears, then the listener quickly brushes it aside, dismissing it as conspiracy or nonsense. The totalitarianism of our censorship happens inside each person. Critical thinking skills are shut off and intellect is replaced with blind conformity and dogmatic loyalty to patriotism, religious ideology, and brand names.

This happens on all sides of the political spectrum. It is the death of democracy. Without dissent and discourse, freedom is a hollow word. Without freedom, there can be no honest democracy. At the trial of democracy's murder, it will be found that a lynch mob beat it to death. The corporate media is guilty. The telecom and tech companies that manipulate search engines and unequal Internet speeds are guilty. The corporations are guilty. The politicians are guilty. And we are guilty.

In an era of uncomfortable truths, the choking of truth is the strangulation of our lives. If we cannot speak about catastrophic, man-made climate change; or the concentration of wealth and simultaneous economic collapse that is impoverishing millions; or the corporate and oligarchic takeover of our country; or the creeping and pervasive spying of the mass surveillance apparatus; or the propaganda and control of corporate advertising; if we cannot speak of and challenge these things, we will continue to die of these injustices. Our death knell is the resounding silence built of censorship and the shrieking sales pitches of profitable lies.

Every human possesses the skills to resist this. We were each born with the ability to shout out that the emperor has no clothes. To speak truth in a time of lies takes courage, but not superhuman powers. We must listen and speak truth. We must discourse – not dismiss – one another. We have to build the means of honest communication. Democracy can be resurrected by breaking silence and listening to complex, uncomfortable truths. Tear your eyes away from mind-numbing sales pitches. There is more to life than blind consumption. We are humans, not locusts. The life of our Earth, our communities, and ourselves, depend on our willingness to break through all forms of censorship and let truth, democracy, and freedom ring.

Rise and Resist

Polite and Apolitical?
Repression By Another Name

Essay Twenty-Seven

There are those who would have us fold up our banners and take down our protest signs. They urge us to be reasonable and polite. They expect us to cram our dissent into narrow boxes of occasional grumbling comments and take our frustration out at the election box once every few years. These people write letters to the editor of small-town newspapers claiming that the visible signs of dissatisfaction – pickets, protesters, political signs – are bad for business and distasteful.

Such sentiments pose great dangers to democracy. Those voices who call for clearing the rabble-rousers from the street fail to perceive that our streets are packed with political messages already. Every corner gas station proudly proclaims its right to destroy our Earth. Every downtown business asserts that commerce is essential and central to community. Each shop selling inoffensive landscape postcards, tourist books, and knickknacks rather than protest banners and political posters is not neutral on the issues. It boldly proclaims that the issues are not as important as maintaining the status quo of business-as-usual.

From such a perspective, our towns and cities are dominated by the political messaging of the supremacy of commerce. When people complain about their fellow citizens holding signs on the street corners, they are, in essence, stating that they believe commerce should have the exclusive right to state its message. This is not democracy. This is totalitarianism.

The right to dissent is essential for functional democracy. Discourse, dialogue, differing views, contention, argument, and the many forms of protest and persuasion are inseparable from a society that can discuss its differences and work toward self-governing resolution. A politely apolitical public society is not neutral; it is enslaved to unstated ideologies, and bound up by cultural apathy and fear. Public space should be as fraught with our differences as the realities of our populace's hearts and minds.

Politeness has devolved from basic respect into a form of repression by which dissent is stifled and silenced. Instead of politeness and propriety, we must embrace the difficult path of honesty and compassion. We must speak truth – for there are hard and painful truths that our nation needs to face – and such truth should be tempered only by our willingness to see the humanity of all people, and to allow our basic compassion and respect to guide our words and actions.

So, go forth with your signs. Lift your banners high. Break silence. Speak out. Fill our streets and public spaces with equal measures of honesty and compassion. Allow the truth to be held up like a mirror to the sickness that ails our society so that they – and we – might understand the reality of what we have become. And, so that they and we can change, heal, and learn to live again.

The Sabotage of Division
(Revolutionary Respect)

Essay Twenty-Eight

Enough! Enough of this senseless criticizing of one another. A Dandelion Insurrectionist who is imprisoned and beaten by the police is no more revolutionary than the mother who gets up in the morning and feeds her child. We all have tasks that are imperatives of our times and we must do them with humility. Those of us trying to make change through civil resistance are no more noble than the plumber trying to clear the shit out of the pipes.

So, enough of this criticizing one another about who is or is not a revolutionary or a radical. Enough name-calling and finger-pointing that someone is a cop-out, or isn't sacrificing enough to the cause, or is playing it too safe, or lacks courage, or is too middle of the road, or too extreme, or too cautious, or too colonized, or too oppressed, or who isn't enough like you to be worthy of your respect.

We will criticize ourselves to death.

We will literally be facing the firing squad, sneering at who flinches, who looks away, who weeps, or who pisses themselves. This animosity toward one another is poisonous. Such malicious judgment cripples our struggle every step of the way. It is shameful; it is laughable. It is certainly not revolutionary.

Using our differences to divide us is an old trick. We love to blame it on our oppressors, but the truth is, it succeeds because we allow it. I have heard the accusations that *They* are dividing us; *They* send undercover agents into our midst to inflame our animosity toward each other. Let me ask you: if the kindling were not laid in our hearts, where would the sparks of division ignite? If you stood ready with the bucket of your awareness and used it douse the smoldering disdain within you, how could their agitation succeed? If we removed the logs and the stones of the fireplace, there would be no place for division to catch fire.

All across the country, this internal scorn is plaguing the Dandelion Insurrection. The radicals sneer at the mainstream; the working class bristles at the academics; the students scoff at the grey-hairs, the elders tear out their thinning hair over the impulsive foolishness of the youth, the spiritual faction derides the shallowness of the non-believers, the secular crowd rolls their eyes at the prayer circles, the communists argue with the capitalists, the socialists turn up their noses at both, the anarchists get haughty at the organizers, the non-profit leaders cringe at the anti-establishment types.

This is no way to run our everyday society, let alone a nonviolent struggle against the powerful corporate-political elite.

There is a place for honest critique, but the use of antagonistic scorn to deride one another is crippling our movement. At this rate, we will be standing on the steps of the Capitol, bitter with each other, jealous of who propelled the final thrust of the movement, suspicious of who will sell-out to the establishment, congratulating our closest

110

companions for their brilliance while secretly sneering *I told you so* at everyone else. Instead of heartfelt celebration at our collective accomplishment, we will be wracked by the same animosity that plagues us now.

At present, however, criticism is so pervasive that our success seems unlikely. Scorn and derision are sabotaging everything we are working toward. Our ability to cooperate is being compromised. Our effectiveness at collaborative strategies is being undermined by our snobbery toward one another.

This must change. We need to practice revolutionary respect for one another. We need to celebrate the contributions of childrearing, garden planting, and protesting equally. Organizing a demonstration is no more important than organizing a prayer vigil. Painting a banner and repainting the local school are both efforts for the wellbeing of all. Hidden in our differences is a beautiful diversity that enriches our lives and expands our minds. Belittling someone for their beliefs, their style of dress, or their political views is limiting and no less discriminatory than sneering at a person's color of skin.

A free, democratic society relies on a respect that extends beyond the *right* to hold views to the *holder* of those views. We have been taught that in order for our belief to be valid, we must stamp out and eliminate all other perspectives. This is tyranny of the mind. Democracy is based on our ability to discuss our differing beliefs without prejudice, to make room in our society for the expression of ideas and opinions, and to respect one another as equals. The equality of a democratic society begins within us. If respect does not blossom there, then it will not be exhibited in our society or government. We must, as Gandhi famously said, be the change we wish to see in the world.

The revolution must begin within each of us.

Pieces of Truth Forged Into Daggers of Deception

Essay Twenty-Nine

When truth and reality are shattered into a thousand shards of deception, skewed and slanted into vicious weapons for power and control, how can we in the Dandelion Insurrection move forward?

Cautiously.

Gandhi said, "We all have a piece of the truth; none of us have the whole truth." Ideally, we would use our diverse perspectives to build a home for all of humanity, a shelter under which we could grow our depth of understanding, and a place where our differences could be addressed and resolved.

That vision has been shattered by those who profit from our animosity.

The rubble of truth is full of broken pieces and dangerous slicing edges. We cut ourselves on half-lies. We shred our flesh on distortions of reality. Slivers of information lodge painfully under our skin and madden us into attacks. Shadowy figures shift the pieces into formations they want us to believe. The glass mosaics are, by turns, haunting, beautiful, seductive, horrifying, and enraging. They pile the pieces of their truths up into walls that seem like solid barriers of reality. We are prodded down cattle chutes of their creation. If we try to

113

escape, we are met by politicians, pundits, or priests wielding long slivers of their particular points-of-view like swords. They slash and whirl in dizzying patterns of persuasion until we are distracted from our search for another path.

Amidst all this, how do we move forward? A wrong step could kill us . . . and wrong steps seem to lie in every direction. Here are a few ways we can begin:

- Don't wield your piece of the truth like a weapon; no matter how "true" you believe it to be. Hold it out, gently, like a dandelion blossom in your hand, for others to see and consider.
- Be skeptical. Be wary. Question everything.
- All pieces of the truth have reasons for their existence. Don't discount them - though don't take them at face value, either.
- Look for why each faction picks up their particular shard of reality. Understand the motives behind every person's perspective.
- Question the patterns and mosaics of truth that people are building. What's being left out? What's being created? What is the reason this version of the truth is being built?
- Think about everything, but be careful about what you project into the world. We don't need more half-truths and speculations flying about.
- Check your facts. Dig to the roots. Uncover the sources.
- Watch out for the craftily-worded ways that people twist the truth.
- Don't be a cog in the gears of the rumor mill.

- Beyond approaching everything with a healthy degree of skepticism and examination, when we do move into action, be sure to put the heart first.
- Love people. (Even the ones you disagree with.)
- Act in tangible ways to take care of people near you. Look after the well-being of your neighborhood. Nourish and sustain life.
- Call for the end of violence and a peace that works toward justice.
- See human beings, not enemies.
- De-escalate animosity. Escalate understanding.
- Withhold judgment. Things are never what they seem.
- Be present. Stay grounded.

And as always, *be kind, be connected, be unafraid!*

Share these ideas with others. Someday, we will rebuild our shared understanding of truth and reality . . . but we cannot do that in the midst of violence, riots, battles, and wars. So, our first step is to teach the Dandelion Insurrection and others to noncooperate with the warmongers who shatter reality into sharp weapons and manipulate us into using truth against one another. Using the tips we just mentioned, we must refrain from a violence built from shards of information and the sharp edges of lies. Everyone must become conscientious objectors to the battle of perspectives. We can de-escalate the conflict by building our awareness and that of others. The shattered world is being used against us. It is time to reach for a deeper understanding of truth.

Rise and Resist

Defending Against the Unknown

Essay Thirty

The challenges that confront us loom imminent, yet still unknown. Like dangers in the dark, we can sense but not clearly see them. Our government is preparing new assaults upon our rights and maneuvering more regressive, unjust legislation through the machine of the political apparatus. The wealthy scheme up new ways to rob and impoverish us. Corporations craft increasing methods by which to profit, even if it means destroying our water, air, land, and health. We are facing dangers on all sides, in shapes and sizes we can barely imagine.

To wait for each new offensive to roll out puts us in a risky and vulnerable position. We must prepare our communities to respond with versatility and courage. In every town, neighborhood, city block, and rural region, we must gather in groups and form strong connections, networks, and coalitions. We need to bring people together to learn the basics of nonviolent struggle, the tactics and types of actions, the strategies and the *how* of what makes it work. We must show the dynamics of participation, noncooperation, repression, and the need for nonviolent discipline.

In our local communities, every member of the Dandelion Insurrection needs to put our golden minds and beautiful heads together. We must articulate the unknown. We must speak the uncertain. We must identify as much as we can about what we think is coming . . . and then we must prepare to meet it.

Craft plans to thwart each threat. Train every member of your community in numerous contingency plans and strategies. From the oldest grandmother to the children who have just learned to read, every person should have knowledge of the many ways we can meet the challenges we might face. Your neighbor should know that if X happens, we will boycott Y. The schoolteachers should be able to explain that if such-and-such a piece of legislation passes, then we will mobilize such-and-such mass civil disobedience against that unjust law. For every possibility, we can prepare a basic strategy of resistance.

And in preparing for the unknown, we become able to confront all possibilities. The muscles of our nonviolent people-power grow in strength. The knowledge of this type of resistance becomes as common as the knowledge of how to use can-openers and light switches. Our leaderless movements transform into *leaderful* movements. Every person knows how to act. We increase the ability of our friends and neighbors to analyze the dangers and strategize effective responses.

As our preparation builds, our well-prepared defense begins to serve as a deterrent against attack. If those who would harm our communities know that we have the ability to thwart them, the chances of their assault decrease. Even if they move ahead, we are now prepared to resist.

We can thank our predecessors for the theory of nonviolent-based defense. To deter fracking, citizens of Quebec strategized and trained their villages to such a degree that the industry was held at bay for over a decade. The gas company had been warned how well-prepared the citizens were to stop them – right down to the dollars and cents it would cost them to "invade". The citizens mapped out roads and rural routes to proposed drilling sites. They planned how and where to launch blockades. They trained hundreds of people in the skills of locking down, setting up roadblocks, peaceful protest, and noncooperation. An emergency phone system was set up to alert citizens if the fracking industry began to drive into the area again. Strategies for banning the gas company from accessing the water sources required for hydraulic fracturing were prepared by both citizens and public officials. An announcement of the millions of dollars, day-by-day, the citizens were prepared to make the gas company pay in delays, fees, and hiring police or other agents of repression was sent to the shareholders and investors in the drilling project.

We need to know our history. Our forbearers in nonviolent struggle gained hard-won lessons that we should learn and apply in our own situations. Far too many struggles failed because they reacted instead of initiated. They allowed the opposition to lead the charge, and never regained the timeline or the high ground of social change. We do not need to wait for what is coming . . . we can rise to meet the times. Like sentinels, we can be watchful, wary, and well prepared.

The Dandelion Insurrection in every corner of this country can train, strategize, mobilize, and stand at ready. Then, our opponents will feel the rumble of our actions. They will hear the roar of our determination rising. The dangers looming in the dark will hesitate.

And if the forces of destruction and injustice dare to launch their attacks, our nonviolent defense will be ready to defeat them.

Rise and Resist

Blockade the Gangplanks On the Titanic

Essay Thirty-One

Blockade the gangplanks of the Titanic! Shut down the boilers of the ship! Storm the stairs from steerage and seize the wheel!

We have passed the point where token victories, small handouts, and crumbs from banquet tables will help us. We have struck too many icebergs. The hull of our society has been breached. Band-Aids on shredded steel will not hold back the floodwaters of injustice.

We are standing on the sinking Titanic. The politicians are huddled in half-empty lifeboats, refusing to come back. They built the ship that's sinking. They mocked the worrywarts who pointed out the lack of lifeboats. They raced full throttle through the dangerous waters, ignoring the looming icebergs of climate change, poverty, economic collapse, growing inequality, fascism, mass surveillance, imperialism, racism, the police state, monopolistic domination, and more. The list of icebergs is too long . . . and we've crashed into them all. We are screaming on the deck, pounding on the windows, thrashing in the black icy waters, or drowned in steerage class, silent and entombed.

The left blames the right. The right accuses the left. Each tells us that if *they* were in charge, this disaster would never have happened.

But they were in charge. Every step of the way, the left and the right were in charge. The disaster happened. They built this ship that's sinking. Stuffed with arrogance and greed, they drove us all to our demise.

Truth is hard. It hurts. It terrifies. But, unlike comforting lies, the truth might set you free. The truth might save our lives.

You must break through the delusion that the oligarchs and corporate pawns will save us. You must starkly confront the terror that all the wealth, power, momentum, steering wheels, boiler rooms, and engines of our nation are in the hands of greed-deluded madmen and fortune-drunk madwomen. You must drop the wishful thinking that they will regulate the Titanic or enforce safety measures or turn a different direction or slow down or fix the ship.

We must save ourselves.

We must organize to blow the whistle on the flawed design plans. We must educate each other of the dangers. We must organize the dockworkers to refuse to load the ship. We must come en masse to block the gangplanks. We must boycott the tickets. We must tell our friends and neighbors to stay off the ship.

Or, if it is too late, if we find ourselves on this metaphorical Titanic, miles out to sea, then we must refuse to load the boilers in the engine room. We must rise up from the lower decks and seize the wheel. We must disrupt the oblivious party on the first-class deck. We must slow the ship to navigate the disasters of these waters.

Bend the metaphor further. Bend it to the breaking point. Dissect the anatomy of disaster. Pick through the pieces of the wreckage of history and learn! Our survival depends on it. How many people must drown in the icy waters before you will drop the comforting lies? Stand and face the truth.

The wealthy politicians and corporate pawns on the left and the right are striking up their marching bands and plastering the town with their posters. They call their ideas unsinkable. They sell us tickets to their Titanic. They want us to believe that if we vote them into power, somehow their flavor of greed will be more palatable as we sink. They promise to reward us by putting us in their lifeboats while the rest of the nation drowns – don't make that devil's pact.

The truth is hard. The truth is painful. The truth is terrifying. But the truth will set you free.

Here is the truth: we must save ourselves. For, if we keep stoking the furnaces of the rich and powerful, we will plow into the final iceberg, sink into the frigid waters, and drown.

Rise and Resist

Rise And Live!

Essay Thirty-Two

Stay asleep, by all means. If you wish to die, sleepwalking over the cliff edge of extinction is one way to go.

Stay afraid, by all means. If you wish to die, cowering in fear until poverty starves or the police state kills you is one way to go.

Stay addicted, by all means. If you wish to die, choking numbed-out and addled by drugs and alcohol is one way to go.

Stay ignorant, by all means. If you wish to die, entering the gas chamber in blissful ignorance is one way to go.

But if you wish to live, you must rise. You must crack open the shell of conformity. You must abandon the wallow of shallow comforts. You must burn, yearn, ache, exalt, weep, laugh, dance, sing . . . you must dare to be alive in the passionate madness that is human life.

The corporate state thrives on your half-dead submission to its domination. It has no heart or soul. So long as you forget yours, the corporate state can keep you slaving for its profits.

But, when the human heart rises like the dawn, when the soul blossoms like a flower, when we awaken, staggeringly alive to our incredible humanness – in these moments the corporate state loses its grip on us. Its control weakens. The hope of humanity's survival appears.

The corporate state is a monstrous being, a person —
supposedly — that does not breathe the air it pollutes, does not
drink the water it poisons, does not give birth to the children
it destroys, does not live as the humans its subjugates. The
corporate state is our familiar, but deadly, demon-ghoul. It is
dead, yet animate; inhuman, yet granted personhood and
enshrined above humans in power, prestige, and importance.

And, so long as we fashion ourselves in the image of the
corporate state, we will be sacrificed to the false god we have
created.

Rise. Live. Explode with the passion, love, vitality, and
complexity that makes you human.

The corporate state has abused humanity and the Earth
for too long. Countless human lives have been thrown into its
ever-hungry jaws. From the dawn of the Industrial Revolution
to today, the monster of the corporate state has swelled in
girth, sprawling massive and destructive across the Earth. It
has tossed us crumbs of comforts so that we will continue to
scurry like ants to gather resources to feed its all-devouring
hunger.

And now humanity is crying, enough! Now the Earth is
screaming, no more! Now, the corporate state strives to
replace biology with wires, emotions with electricity, and
humans with robots. When we rebel, we are replaced by the
armies of automation, soulless spawn of the corporate state
that will never resist its greedy cruelties. As in the early days
of the Industrial Revolution, machines are sold to the
unwitting as humanity's liberation. We will have so much free
time, they say, no one will have to slave away and work all
day. And yet, we should know how this sales pitch ends: as in
the past, humanity will either be tied back to production lines

and profits by economic necessity . . . or we will be starved as "obsolete" and "expendable". The corporate state will replace humanity with programmable, unfeeling computers that will supplant and suppress the natural rebellion of the human heart.

This is what we face. It is a struggle of frightening proportions, one that dwarfs all epics of olden times. Every human being must declare our independence from the corporate state. We must hold our truths, self-evident. We must sing our bodies, electric. We must lift our naked hairiness to the sky. We must be phenomenal women – and men – and rise to live as all our poets dreamed. We must feel the whole earth crying, calling us to our hearts and souls, reminding us of our origins. We have no life without this Earth. We are bundles of carbon, oxygen, water, flesh, blood, heart, soul, mind, emotions, memories, and imagination. We are beautiful, incredible, and irreplaceable.

But, if we do nothing, the corporate state will kill us, along with millions of other species. It will leave computers and robots ruling over the dwindling population of human beings. We will be left either denying our flesh-and-blood, or being oppressed beyond the endurance of the human heart and soul.

If humanity is to live, we must rise.

Rise and Resist

We are Hurtling Toward Death; Step Out of Line and Resist

Essay Thirty-Three

Muster courage to resist. Outrage is a mere spark; it must ignite the flame of courageous determination or else its light dies swiftly. You will need the stronger fuels of love, hope, and vision to sustain you through the struggle.

Build up your muscles for the marathon of change. Drill and train. Focus your mind. Release the illusion that a normal life is possible. It's not. Life-as-usual is a race toward extinction. You may not be the first lemming toppling off the cliff's edge, but you will hurtle over by the time this madness of endless profit-driven growth is done. We must break the chains of expectations and turn the strides of our life in a different direction.

When all of life is at stake, our lives must be thrown into resistance to tip the scales of the world toward life. Assess the patterns of your day-to-day life. If you find yourself spending more time watching movies than at organizing meetings, make a shift. Show up at protests more regularly than parties. Participate in boycotts, strikes, and divestment campaigns as often as you go to the grocery store, the bank, or the post office. Train for change as frequently as you exercise your body.

The pull of normalcy and the status quo is strong. Like an

undertow, it will try to drag you under and suck you back into the current of our destructive culture. Floating along in complacency is a sure way to be thrust over the waterfall onto the smashing rocks below. You must swim against the current of what our society, workplaces, entertainment, and advertisements call normal. Everything will try to drag you back in line with enticements, burdens, debts, pressures, warnings, and even threats. But remember where this culture is headed: we are hurtling toward death. You must have the courage to step out of line and resist.

Hope, love, and vision can strengthen you for the struggle. A few good friends can thwart the loneliness of the path. Clarity – inner and outer – can bolster you against the mockery of others and defy those who call you crazy for speaking truth about our dire situation.

Our lives – and the future of the Earth – depend on your courage to resist. Cultivate the fuels that can sustain the sparks of outrage and propel us through the long haul of the struggle we face. Shift the pattern of your life into training and action. Remember that many others are striving to do this as well. Across the country in the hearts and minds of thousands, people like you are turning against the tide, swimming against the current, breaking free of the stampede, and racing toward the chance of life!

Resisting Operation Extract & Export

Essay Thirty-Four

Don't wait until the perils of extraction are on your doorstep, in your backyard, or poisoning your water. Look around! Pay attention to the stories coming from the north, south, east, and west. See the hard truth: the noose is tightening.

Oil and gas extraction is invading the United States of America, occupying this country like a foreign power comprised of global elites and wealthy interests. Every pipeline, drilling rig, and export terminal is funded by a transnational alliance of greedy crooks and criminals wearing the facade of respectability, big name banks, and brand-recognition corporate logos.

These are the ideological descendants of the war criminals of human history: the tyrants, dictators, genocidal maniacs, supremacists, and conquistadors. They are the Hannibals and Genghis Khans and King George's. They are the modern empire builders . . . and they are here to pillage and plunder, murder, rape, and destroy.

They have spewed lies for decades and brainwashed half our populace. They have produced pseudo-science denying climate change to mislead our citizens. They continue to claim their oil and gas developments are for *energy independence* when the track record of pipelines, export terminals, and financiers is clear: they have seized power to extract and export our resources, against our will, and to line their own pockets.

As the world's nations shift toward renewables and ban fossil fuel extraction within their lands, a dangerous race is going on. Like teenagers with cars, the fossil fuel addicts are playing chicken. They are driving full-throttle to the cliff's edge of extinction, believing that he who laughs last, laughs best. Whichever set of extractors holds the final fossil fuel card stands to win enormous profits in the era of expensive fossil fuel pricing. So, the greedy elites who occupy our halls of power are engaged in *Operation Extract and Export*. The United States is the cash cow of their greed as they mine the resources beneath the surface and sell them overseas.

We have been invaded, conquered and colonized once again. The irony of the situation stabs like a knife to the gut. Americans are descendants of centuries of conquest and genocide. The biggest bullies have always risen to the top. Now, we are all being subjugated again. Long ago, the colonial pillage was for gold, timber, furs, and land. Today, the violence and repression is to steal the oil and gas that will poison and pollute every inch of its journey from its rise to the surface to the pipelines across the landscape to the end users and the emissions released into the air. Our water, air, land, and entire planet will be destroyed by this greed.

We must rise up to stop it.

Three hundred and twenty million souls stand between this destructive greed and the beautiful fragile living Earth we inhabit. But many are passive, brainwashed, addicted to fossil fuels, in denial of climate change, bought off by the grimy lint of deep pockets, deluded by lies about energy independence, irrationally afraid of the Chinese, Saudis, Russians, or whichever bogeyman of the day has been dredged up to keep the populace in line.

As for the rest of us . . . we must throw our lives into active nonviolent resistance. There is no other option. The oil and gas elites control the left and the right of our politics, which is nothing more than the apparatus of wealthy pillaging and plunder. They control the courts, which have, year-by-year, decision-by-decision, built up the right of corporations over the rights of people and never granted the rest of the Earth, animals, plants, or ecosystems any rights whatsoever. There are no knights in shining armor looming on our horizon. We must do the hard, determined work of not only stopping pipelines and extraction, but taking back our democracy as well.

In politics, culture, knowledge, media, entertainment, social circles, education, finance, business – in every sector of our nation, we must wrest back popular power, and insist on shared decision-making by and of the People. We must actively build true democracy, in politics *and* in every other aspect of our lives. Every pipeline, oil rig, gas well, and export terminal must be resisted. We have to organize campaigns to divest every dollar possible. We have to stop banks and investors from profiting off the most destructive and dangerous industry on the planet. We must mobilize in our towns and communities for renewable energy and conservation.

And, on top of all this, we must declare the truth: we have been invaded and occupied by greedy elites and corporate power. We can no longer accept this situation; we must change it. We must reject, actively, their lies and brainwashing. We must evict them from our halls of power.

And we must do this today, not tomorrow. We must act now . . . before we no longer have clean water to drink or air to breathe or a healthy planet that we can call home.

Where Is Your Loyalty?

Essay Thirty-Five

For all the avowed patriots who demand my Pledge of Allegiance and salutes on Loyalty Day, Fourth of July, and other patriotic, militarized holidays, I fling this question to your hearts: how deep and far does your loyalty to your country run?

Our culture applauds those who risk their lives in battlefields, allegedly defending our country in wars that we later understand to be for the profits of privileged elites. Our loyalty to our country appears to stop there. Our national celebrations of loyalty and service are charades. They demand loyalty of all citizens by demonstrating our loyalty to our military and politicians. But where is the loyalty to our fellow citizens who are suffering? When do we honor that?

What is love of one's country if not a love that extends beyond ideals and platitudes to weep over the injustices and harms experienced within our nation? Is it love to stay silent when remediable suffering abounds? Is it devotion to allow the children of our nation to lack potable drinking water while billions are spent on more weaponry?

My love – and loyalty to – my country is not a set of slogans, lofty skyscrapers, or staggering stockpiles of wealth. No, my love of my country is courageous enough to include the broken and hurting places; the weeping rivers contaminated with coal sludge; the infants who die early from fracking contaminants; the veterans wracked unto suicide with the horrors they've experienced; the poor thrown out of homes, onto the streets, driven out of towns to die in the margins. My country is large enough to include every inch of our lands with an unflinching gaze, seeing the prosperous and plighted, greedy and generous, alike.

My loyalty resides in tending to the least of us, the most abused and broken-hearted, the marginalized, and the forgotten. A country is not a standard of measurement by which some are damned and excluded, and others are accepted and exalted. A nation is a promise, a commitment to all those born on its soil and all those who join later in life, that we will bear a tender responsibility to one another, that we will care for one another, that we will help one another through life. Our nation fails, again and again, to live up to this. My heart aches for this failing, as well. That is what loyalty does: it holds up our potential and calls us back to it unceasingly no matter how much we err.

My love of my country cannot be symbolized by flags and parades and uniforms and speeches, for it extends far beyond the confines of humanity. Every stream, lake, ocean shore, forest, field, mountain; the bears, eagles, moose, wolves, coyotes, foxes, whales, dolphins, salmon, catfish, lobster, rabbit, mouse, ant, centipede; every beast and being of this land demands our loyalty as well.

And when I am slapped with the demand for patriotic loyalty and unquestioning obedience to authorities, I turn my other cheek and ask: where then is our loyalty to democracy? That which questions, critiques, dissents? Where is our loyalty to the rest of our people, the ones who suffer in our streets? Where is our loyalty to our land and waters, that which builds the very firmament of our being?

Do not throw the shallow loyalty of puppets and politicians at me! It reeks of greed and hypocrisy. It smacks of coercion and deception. It stinks of lies and manipulation.

My loyalty runs as deep as the oceans, wide as the great vast sky that stretches across our country. It refuses to look away from the suffering of any inch of our nation: human, animal, plant, mineral, elemental. It stands at the sickbed of those without healthcare. It bears witness to the people shot in the streets. It remembers the hidden millions in prisons. It starkly sees the cruelties of moguls, magnates, and tycoons. It aches as the waters of this nation are poisoned. It weeps as the great mountains are blasted to bits.

A loyalty un-blinded rages at the injustices of this country; it holds the feet of power holders to the fire of truth; it dares to critique, to dissent, to speak out . . . indeed, it does not dare be silent.

When someone you love is in danger, or causes injustice and great harm to others, your loyalty demands that you act to dissuade them from the path that they're on, and return them to sanity, awareness and compassion.

That is my loyalty to my country, that I will speak out against our wrongdoings and cruelties; that I will dissent from the demand for unquestioned obedience to authority; that I will love my country so ferociously that I will not allow us to remain complacent, nor deluded by the addiction to power and control; that I must speak for the other species that share our geography; and that I will include, unflinchingly, the face of every human being who lives here in my definition of my country. Such is my loyalty. Such is my love.

Rise and Resist

The Empire Has No Clothes

Essay Thirty-Six

The empire has no clothes. Be the boy who dares to speak the truth: there is no democracy. All around you, the courtiers are clapping and cheering, but their trembling hands are showing. They are terrified to admit the truth. There is no democracy in the US empire; rich people and corporations run the show. Study after study has shown this. The courtiers of power have been applauding the empire for so long, they're afraid to speak the truth. But you cannot afford to let yourself be fooled. The empire has no clothes. There is no democracy in the Unites States.

The clever tailors have done their legwork. They have millions of people convinced. The empire stands naked, clothed only in the hype, rumors, lies, platitudes, empty speeches, false words, and illusions about democracy. On the left of the empire stands the Democratic Party. On the right stands the Republicans. In between them is the naked empire, cloaked in the finest "robes" of lies and buzz words. It is a hideous, terrifying sight. Parts of the naked empire are bloated. Others emaciated to the bone. Sores fester. Wounds bleed. Pustules burst. The empire stands rank and deluded – even those whose eyes are open wish we could cover up this shame.

Those clever two-party tailors (and the empire) have convinced everyone that we must applaud the non-existent democracy or you'll have your head chopped off. The executioners wear the hooded masks of our fears: terrorists, foreigners, immigrants, tree-huggers, liberals, conservatives, racists, bleeding hearts, poverty, taxes, economic collapse, police, bankers – the list is endless and ever-changing. It serves to keep us terrified into playing the two-party game. That's the trick to executioners' hoods: they hide the truth. Anyone could be underneath that mask, and the clever tailors have us each hoodwinked by our fears.

Frightened, we play along. We clap our hands for the naked empire. We pretend it still has democracy. We keep repeating what the courtiers of power say: get out and vote, call your reps, sign petitions. If the empire *actually* had clothes, if it *actually* had a shred of functional democracy (or decency) left, then these actions would be as sensible as admiring the fabric of a new coat or the lace trim on a sleeve. Perhaps not enough, given the circumstances of the multiple crises crashing into our lives, but not delusional. Unfortunately, the practices of democracy are no longer grounded in any functional truth.

The clever tailors of the two-party system are profiting from maintaining the charade. They're growing rich by convincing us that it's democracy they're weaving on their loom. They're stitching together the semblance of democracy with candidates and platforms. They're hemming (and hawing) about democracy in congress and committees. They're pantomiming an incredible show, snipping at nothing and sewing up hot air. And the mighty empire is nodding its head. After all, this charade is all that keeps the people quiet. This illusion of democracy keeps the people from revolting. It stops us from joining nonviolent movements for change. It keeps our resources of time and money caught up in buying the two-party tailors invisible thread and see-through fabric in which to drape the empire. The show keeps us from putting our own hands to the warp and weft of democracy and from picking up the needle, thread, and scissors. We could be determining the pattern and style of our political process. We could be crafting a type of democracy that fits our collective body politic. But the clever tailors have stolen the show. Their ruse keeps us from taking power.

Dare to be the boy who calls the bluff. Say it clearly: the empire has no democracy. Get up in the morning and remind yourself – you can be sure that many will try to convince you otherwise throughout the day.

From this essential admission of the honest truth, we must go to work. We must use the tools of nonviolent action to change the fabric of the nation. Thread by thread, we must weave and spin, trim and stitch, hem and cut this nation into the style of politics we need.

You may find, in this process, that the empire itself comes unraveled. The two-party tailors collapse. The courtiers spin in confusion and squawk in fear. The hoods of the executioners come off. Hold fast. Stay focused. Keep creating true democracy. Sew the clothes on your own back. Let our communities wear the mantle of democracy, all of us, together.

Rise and Resist

After the Vote

Essay Thirty-Seven

The Vote – the beloved, abused, scorned, corrupted, stolen, hijacked, pointless, profound, hopeful, depressing, hard-won, cherished vote – is not the only way to take action for meaningful change. Currently, the elections operate in our nation like a cattle chute, all too often forcing us back into the deadly, no-win tracks of a two-party duopoly that serves only the moneyed class. It becomes a handy device for siphoning off the demand for revolutionary change by giving false hope that elected officials will actually enact their campaign promises once in office.

Instead of taking matters into our own, capable, millions of hands, we vote to let someone else take care of it. And, in large part, these representatives do nothing. We wind up hamstringing our movements over and over. We vote for Candidate X's promises of someday guaranteeing living wages – instead of going on strike until we actually get them. We vote for Candidate Y's vow to someday ban assault weapons – instead of picketing and blockading arms dealers. Instead of targeting fossil fuel investors, we try to elect politicians to craft legislation that, even if passed, is largely ignored by industry until they manage to get officials and judges in place to overturn the law.

It is maddening and infuriating. We have other – and better – options.

Change happens on many levels: cultural, economic, industrial, social, artistic, personal, psychological, spiritual, and more. We must work in all of them if we hope for lasting, systemic shifts. Don't be fooled by the annual circus of voting. Go vote, sure, but don't sit back down on the couch once you've cast your ballot. Go out into your community, businesses, churches, colleges, and so on, and work for the changes we wish to see in the world. In truth, no legislation has the power to enact the full scope of change without the cooperation of all those other institutions and the popular support in ordinary citizens.

Want living wages, for example? Change the sickening culture of greed and the hero worship of the criminals at the top of capitalism's cannibalistic food chain. Challenge the moral "right" our culture places upon exploitation and survival of the fittest. We will never see justice for workers while we salivate over billionaires and laud their "brilliance" with which they "made their fortunes". This "brilliance" is ruthless willingness to shove others under the bus. Their "fortunes" were stolen from others by means of low wages, high prices, global exploitation, insider deals, destruction of the earth, corruption of democracy, and self-serving laws and legislation.

Elections and politics are the games of elites. We are whipped up each election cycle to serve as the cheering crowds at their jousting matches. It is no better than the feudal days of fighting for this king or that queen when the real struggle is the establishment of "nobles" and the theft of common land from the people. In the 1500s, the real struggle was not whether Queen Elizabeth of England or Mary Queen of Scots would sit on the throne, but rather, how ordinary women were being stripped of rights and lowered into the status of property. Neither Mary nor Elizabeth's rule stopped the rise of patriarchy into the monstrous beast that still roars in the policies and practices of today.

History is long; I could go on with examples across nations, class, and creed. The real challenge of our times is not which super-wealthy right or left-leaning regime gets to hand out sweet deals to their cronies, but how we, the People, wrest the state apparatus from the death-grip of the "nobility" of our times. Just as fighting for this king or that queen was not as important as defending the commons, so do I warn you today not to over-inflate the significance of the vote.

The idea is wonderful; our practice of it, deplorable. Never confuse those two. Prize our ideals. Exercise your right to vote – it is hard-won for most of our populace - but never allow its current, corrupted incarnation to distract you from working on cultural, economic, social, or any other type of change. Measure for measure, pour your courageous heart into all levels of change. If you spend ten minutes reading a report about a candidates' forum, spend the same time reading about – and participating in – strikes for better wages or sit-ins to abolish mass incarceration or shut-downs of insurance offices for affordable healthcare. If you go door-to-door canvassing for a politician, spend an equal amount of time knocking on doors to build support for a boycott of exploitative goods. If you're willing to throw a house party for an election campaign, go to a local organizer and offer to throw a house party in support of their social justice cause. If you donate to a political campaign, donate to a movement, too.

These are just a few examples. Remember that the elections have become a massive industry. Meanwhile, many of our social justice movements are run by miracle-workers working on shoestring budgets. Your time, skills, and donations are all deeply appreciated by your fellow citizens who are striving for significant change. Don't forget them during the shouting matches of our election circuses. Without our movements changing the hearts and minds and daily lives of ordinary people, the mere words on paper that make up legislation have no meaning. Laws are irrelevant if officials ignore them, courts reject them, and people disobey them. Do the legwork of making sure that the populace can uphold justice, not merely because it is the law, but because it is our will, our belief, and our sense of justice turned into a way of life. To do this, you must make change in every level of our lives.

A Revolution of Democracy

Essay Thirty-Eight

What do we do when we finally understand that the elections really are stolen? Or rigged? Or thrust out of our reach by the manipulations of rich and powerful people? Corrupted by corporations? How long does it take before we call the bluff? Another disappointing election cycle? Two? Three? How much more gerrymandering, corporate buying of elections, voter disenfranchisement, and outright fraud can we stand? When will we take seriously the necessity of change?

This is not a democracy of, for, and by the people. And at the rate we're going, it never will be.

We cannot, as many claim, vote our way into power when no aspect of the two-party duopoly represents anything other than elite interests. The system is designed to empower rich people and their massive corporations, no one else. Over the years, it has been modified to allow different faces to represent it, but the agenda has stayed much the same.

We must see the system in all its cruelty and injustice. We must be brave enough to surrender our false hopes and wistful ideals about it. From 1787 onward, this government has been designed to serve the privileged, to reinforce such privilege, and to protect the "property" of the wealthy class, including at one point, women and African-Americans.

It's high time for that to change.

We, the people, were never asked, back in 1787, what sort

of government we'd like. Only a scant handful of people from a mere 6% of the populace (white, propertied males) were invited to vote on the Constitution. The rest of us have struggled for freedom and power ever since.

Perhaps it's time to have that much-belated conversation about the kind of government we'd prefer to participate within. (Undoubtedly, a pay-to-play elections process requiring millions and billions of dollars is not high on the list of ideas for the average, broke American.) We, the People, are long overdue for a deep, revolutionary discussion about what sort of decision-making structures we want to see in our world. And, it's time for a serious nationwide movement for democracy, with all the breadth and depth of possibility the phrase entails.

Democracy is not merely a form of government. It must be a way of life, a set of ethics and an ethos of a culture. For functional democracy to arise, it must be a widespread practice in our work, schools, homes, businesses, markets, religious institutions, and social clubs. We must strive to understand the spirit of the word, not merely the *form* of the word as embodied by the process of voting every few years for a representative.

We must dare to dream in the complex intricacies of what we don't know about democracy. We must study democracy like a foreign language, learning processes like sentence structures, practicing our articulation, searching for the words to describe what we mean when we cry for democracy. We must examine the immense richness of humanity's many experiments in shared decision-making and become familiar with the successes, failures, and potential pitfalls.

We must also break free of the conditioning of

disempowerment and dare to imagine what decision we might make – for good or for ill – if we, together, designed our society, politics, economics, and culture. Democracy in any format requires a revolutionary re-envisioning of our way of life. A nation of brow-beaten workers, automatons, consumers, and bosses will never succeed in functional democracy. A real democracy requires a broad spectrum of humanity to show up with all our varied talents, skills, and perspectives: dreamers, artists, engineers, mothers and fathers, scientists, doctors, lovers, students, and more. In short, it takes us all to discover what will work for us all.

It will take love; and the foundation of love, respect. Democracy, as is so-often said, is more than two cats and a mouse deciding what's for dinner. Indeed, it is. We must explore that "more" and illuminate what is required. We need to make vast changes in how we create media, entertainment, education, and public discourse in order to find the practices that best serve to foster understanding and conflict resolution. We need to increase the types of cultural experiences that move us toward loving and caring for our fellow citizens, rather than hating and fearing them. Real democracy requires levels of knowledge, compassion, and respect that we, as a nation, have never practiced before. Here then, lies the groundwork of our democratic revolution: we must build the respect among ourselves by which a real democracy can hear and meet its peoples' needs.

For we are talking about a revolution. It might be nonviolent in nature, but its scope is a massive upheaval, not just in politics, but in society and culture as well. Make no mistake: our culture is far from democratic. Even overhauling the injustices that burden the current political apparatus would require revolutionary changes. An effort that seeks not just minor adjustments, but a profound re-envisioning in the ways we make every decision in our lives is nothing short of a revolution. It should be treated and understood as such. We should prepare ourselves for the reality of demanding such change. We must gird ourselves for the struggle if we ever wish to see government of, by, and for the people, all of us, together.

The Government Ain't Your Daddy

Essay Thirty-Nine

The government is not your father. The mega-corporations that monopolize your sustenance are not your mother. Obedience to their abuse is inappropriate … it is time to stop obeying. Imagine what you know is true: elections are a sham. Our politicians are not related to us by vote. They treat us all like bastards. The corporations that we expect to feed us, clothe us, shelter us, and provide for us are not our parents. We were adopted for a moment, when we had cash inside our pockets, but now we're useless to them – worse than useless; we're sick and weak and cannot do their work. The corporations are through with us. We're being abandoned on the roadside.

It has been said many times that America is in its adolescence. We are immature, pimply, self-indulgent, egocentric creatures. We conceal our insecurity in arrogance. We cover cowardice with bravado. Responsibility is ignored as we indulge in video games, sex, drugs, alcohol, chips and soda pop.

Watch out, then, for time holds still for no one. Pain and suffering force rapid growth and the average American crashing through folly toward maturity. As our country confronts rising rates of poverty (approaching nearly fifty percent by international standards), we are no longer the teenage inheritors of the earth with keys to shiny cars and proms, college educations, and suburban houses with white picket fences. We are not the children of a dream, but young adults confronted with a harsh reality. Our national household contains our dying mothers riddled with cancer, our hungry baby sisters, our laid-off fathers, our ailing grandparents, our meth-addicted younger brothers, and our incarcerated cousins.

We are scrambling to keep ourselves alive.

And this government that claims to know what's best is beating us in its drunken stupor. The profit-addicted corporations are feeding arsenic to the baby. We hear the slurred and senseless speeches of this government and a hot surge of resentment chokes us. We struggle to hold our family together while the corporations take the lunch money from the children to get high on the drug of war. We stare dumbfounded, as the corporate government demands our obedience. These false parents are ordering us to get into the car that will drive us off the cliff of climate change.

Obedience to this abuse is not a virtue.

With the ferocious force of youthful rebelliousness burning in our chests, we must grab our little sister, sling the baby on our hip, and refuse to let these people order us around. A government that does not serve its people does not deserve allegiance. Authority that abuses its position forfeits its right to our obedience. Entities that rob and poison people, rape the land and plunder public money should no longer enjoy our cooperation with such destruction.

We cannot obey them and survive.

We must grow up rapidly and painfully. Our government does not watch over us. It takes our last remaining dollar and gives it to the thugs of the military-industrial complex. It convinces us to resent our feeble grandmothers and starving children while it parties with the good ole boys. We must confront these lies! We must say to them, *do not try to make us hate our people. The poor are not the robbers of our hard-earned money. You are! You give a penny to the old people and drink the rest in subsidies to your corporate cronies! You buy million-dollar drones while the children have no winter coats! Your gorge yourself on opulence while the people scrounge in dumpsters for their food!*

And when the government punches you for your outburst, look up, young teenager; look up with your bloody nose and blackened eye!

"Don't get fresh," the government will say.

And with fire burning in your eyes, you'll think: *I'm not. I'm getting wise.*

The government is still larger, stronger, more experienced and tougher than you . . . but you are getting wise. You won't fight him with fists or knives or guns . . . he'll always beat you at that game. Instead, you'll learn his weaknesses: where he goes to drum up money, which of his thugs resents his brutal abuses, what groups he leans on for support, and who among your brothers and sisters won't take his bullying anymore. One by one, you'll gather allies, erode his support, and cut him off. No one will give him money. No one will include him in the deals. No one allows him to crash their parties, sleep with their wives, take their cars and crash them. One by one, you strengthen the people and remove their unwitting obedience to abuse. You strengthen their pride in themselves, their ability to care for one another, and the resilience of their communities. You tell them that real fathers and mothers are people who care for the weak and immature. Fathers and mothers are flesh-and-blood human beings with hearts and souls. Corporations cannot replace them. Tyrants cannot take their place. Governments should not expect the obedience we gave to our parents when we were young. Americans are not children. We are adults, equals among equals. As friends and neighbors, we can govern ourselves.

The abuses of the government and the corporations are unfortunate, but let us not bemoan the loss of hierarchical control. Whether the tyrants are benevolent or destructive, they still usurp the right to self-governance that exists in every human being. Respect demands that we cease treating full-grown adults as subordinates to be ruled over. The long arc of civil and equal rights that granted suffrage and liberty to women, African-Americans, and all classes must be carried further. America must leave its adolescent reliance on representative politicians who do nothing but abuse us. We must grow into fully functional adults who can work together to provide for our whole society.

We must look around at other nations, our neighbors on this planet, and instead of attacking them, we must learn from them, strengthen them, and support one another as we deal with catastrophic climate change, collapsing economies, and political instability. We are heaving in the agonies of coming of age on this planet, but beyond the pain of growing up is a long life for this human species ... a long life that we won't survive to enjoy if we obey our profit-addicted, abusive government and corporations. We must disobey, break the rules, and evoke the rebellion of the teenager to grow into the maturity of the adult. We must trust our innate sense of injustice. We must have faith in our ability to create something brighter from the ashes of the old. We must find the courage to change the course of our lives.

The Laboratory of Democracy

Essay Forty

The United States is a laboratory for democracy – a centuries-long experiment in what does and does not work for people making decisions together. Our experimental efforts have often been thwarted by undemocratic interests. Moments of abject failure and soaring success punctuate long periods of disruption, shut-downs, and the regular ransacking of our laboratory. Over and over, the equipment has been smashed or corrupted. The results have been ripped to shreds. The data has been distorted. The facilities have been destroyed. The funding has been cut off. Every aspect of our experiment in democracy has been tampered with by those who fear the will of the people.

Our research has been pilloried by moneyed interests, leading to misconceptions about democracy. People mock what they do not understand. They equate democracy with mere majoritarian electoral politics, or the dismal status quo of politics in the United States. Democracy is a far vaster, extraordinary field of experimentation, vibrant ideas, unusual practices, and effective tools for shared decision-making and collective self-governance. The practice of democracy engages listening, respect, justice, equality, dialogue, caring, compassion, creativity, shared decision-making, collective strategizing, and conflict resolution. It appears as participatory budgeting, collective public policy crafting, civic dialogues, community discussion practices, ranked choice voting, direct democracy, citizen initiatives, cooperative structures, and much more.

If we wish to cast off the shackles of tyranny, the chains of autocratic control, the burden of massive monopolies, the constraints of totalitarianism, and the rule of corporate or oligarchic interests, then we must learn the language of democracy as an ever-evolving poetry of politics. Democracy is more than a noun, it should be a verb, an active practice of shared governance. And, as we resist the injustice of a corporate-controlled state, we must broaden our very definition of democracy.

The old practices of politics allowed this collusion of corporations, rich people, and state power to abuse people and planet. Our democracy must rise in newer, more robust forms reaching into every sector of our governance, whether it be political, social, economic, or otherwise. Democracy is a way of life, not simply voting on candidates every few years.

We must push our experiments in democracy beyond the known parameters. Looking to the past will not offer us answers for the complexity of today. The Founding Fathers could only see as far as the horizon-lines of their prejudices. They could not imagine the world we live in now, one in which people of color, women, and minorities of every persuasion demand a system of governance that is inclusive, responsive, and responsible to and for the well-being and equality of every citizen, the natural world, and our fellow humanity around the globe.

Even in the history of the United States, our notion of politics has been broadened time and time again. Mass movements for greater equality and inclusion began almost as soon as the ink dried upon the Constitution. The United States has always been a work in progress. We must look around at what our fellow humans are doing in places where they have outstripped our inquiries into democracy. We must also look to the unknown and the imagined. We must study the possibilities and implement them as experimental practices to build upon.

The United States is a laboratory of practice. As we dethrone the corporate state and rule of the rich, we must also rebuild this laboratory, pick up the wreckage, set up new tests, repair equipment, celebrate discoveries, and fund further investigations. Such inquiry must be the bastion of our efforts to discover the true meaning of democracy; of governance of, by, and for the people, all of them, together.

Rise and Resist

Constitution 2.0

Essay Forty-One

If we, the people, wrote a constitution now, what would go in it? Equal rights for women, men, non-binary, and undefined? Caps on wealth tied to poverty levels? Rights of nature? Reparations for past crimes, wrongs, and thefts? Limits on military spending? A free and open Internet? Abolition of mass incarceration or the replacement of the entire prison system with restorative and community justice? Free healthcare for all? Living wages or universal basic income? Would we keep corporate personhood or the electoral college?

The possibilities are endless; they include a million ideas over which to agree or vehemently oppose. We can envision things (like airplanes, climate change, and the Internet) beyond the Founding Fathers' wildest dreams . . . and that is exactly the point of even raising the question of a Constitution 2.0. Our first constitution was written by propertied white men to the exclusion of all others, centuries ago when messages traveled by horseback and 94% of the population was excluded from all political process. Like an aging computer program, we've patched in updates over the years, but perhaps it's time to overhaul the operating system and redesign it to reflect the dreams, needs, interests, and ideas of 100% of us.

The US Constitution was designed to empower and serve

property and wealth. It is unresponsive to the demands and plights of ordinary people. It often fails to incorporate concerns beyond those of commerce, wealth, and property. The Bill of Rights was added as a protest by constitutional delegates who were alarmed by the earlier drafts. Small protections like the EPA, the Clean Air & Water Act, and the FDA are vulnerable to corruption and dismantlement by hostile administrations. The Declaration of Independence's revolutionary proclamation of the inalienable right to "life, liberty, and pursuit of happiness" was shifted in the Constitution to preserving the rights of an elite to "life, liberty, and protection of property". Ever since then, we have struggled to update the US Constitution to reflect the needs of its people. Perhaps it's time for a Constitution 2.0.

I am not recommending that we completely throw out the old and rush a new political operating system into existence. (No software designer would advise that approach.) This creates power vacuums that are inevitably exploited by the most depraved, opportunistic, piratical, and tyrannical bullies. No, I am instead recommending that we allow the potential of a nationwide re-imagining of our governing documents to throw open the doors of civic conversation . . . and let our dreams break free of the corsets that bind our imagination and suffocate our political aspirations.

We risk our lives for mere crumbs, waging struggle for the chance to glean the leftovers from the plutocrats' feasts, or lick the floors under their groaning tables. We deserve to dream larger. We should organize to build, seize, and run the bakeries, kitchens, farms, delivery systems, grocery stores, and warehouses by which the daily bread of our lives is given shape and form. We have been trained to petition for scraps like pleading beggars rather than seizing the means of destiny, existence, and self-governance.

I dare you to lift your eyes and dream like the magnificent human being that you are: one among many, each equal to the other, none above or below the next.

I call for a Constitution 2.0 because the old document – and all of its revisions right up until today – was written by a narrow elite with only partial enfranchisement of our citizenry. We have never imagined what all 320 million of us might craft as a governing structure. Would mothers and fathers demand veto power over the wars their children are sent to fight in? Would students demand referendum rights on whether our budget should be spent on education or military? Would seniors insist on basic incomes and affordable healthcare so they can live their elder years in ease, contributing their skills and wisdom to our communities? We cannot answer these questions in and through our current political system. What would a Constitution 2.0 look like if it was designed to empower (not limit) widespread political participation?

Never in the history of the United States have we recognized the shared humanity of one another and cultivated the respect and trust that we would need to write a Constitution 2.0. Nor am I foolish enough to assume that we have those skills now. A constitutional convention (as imagined by the Founding Fathers) would most likely devolve into a brawl, a civil war, an oligarchic coup, or worse.

Democracy of, by, and for the people cannot be crafted overnight. It is a mass endeavor, one that spans the scope of years, and is designed to engage our citizenry in a multitude of ways. Creativity, visioning, education, knowledge-sharing, communication, dialog, and exploration would all be needed. Healing, truth-telling, and connection are all necessary for a populace as deeply wounded and divided as ours. When I call for a Constitution 2.0, I am asking not just for a final document, but a collection of processes by which we, in pursuit of shared ideals, forge a more perfect union than the original framers of the US Constitution could ever envision. We have no chattel slavery anymore, though racism continues to plague our land. Women are no longer property, though neither are they treated as men's equals. The child is no longer a creature "to be seen and not heard", but a treasure unfolding over time, offering insights and gifts of their own. The LGBTQ community is coming out of closets and shadows and the margins of society where centuries of persecution has pushed them for too long. The Earth is demanding that we listen and treat the living systems with respect. So much has shifted since the late 1700s. We must update our operating system to keep pace.

While it is foolhardy to imagine that our populace could enter a room without dealing with the harms of the past, present, and future; it is also inaccurate to assume that we are incapable of undergoing a transformative process in pursuit of a Constitution 2.0. Such a goal requires a realistic assessment of the resources we need, the pitfalls and sabotages of the processes, and the depth of understanding, truth-telling, growth, knowledge-sharing, and healing that would facilitate an effective redesign of our governing structure. We need to call upon our institutions to play a supportive role instead of a destructive, dominating, or manipulative role.

We must ask ourselves: what might we do to prepare the entire populace for such a revolutionary, inspiring, and

162

terrifying endeavor? After centuries of abuse, oppression, injustice, inequality, and suffering, how would we heal enough of our wounds to even discuss the crafting of a new constitution with each other? Backloads of lies and propaganda need to be cleared out. Truth-tellings could be held (perhaps every day in every town for the next decade). Story circles could be facilitated to help us learn to look into the eyes of our fellow citizens and start to hear and know each other beyond the stereotypes perpetuated in the fear-mongering and power-hoarding media apparatus of elites. The information bubble that hovers unseen over the United States needs to be burst so the bright ideas and best practices from around the world can be seen and shared. Knowledge must be spread of participatory, direct, wise, and real democracy; horizontal organizing, sociocracy, the commons, collective processes, and so much more. Trainings on how to hold a discourse (rather than a shouting match) need to become as common as driver's education courses.

To even raise these ideas is undoubtedly considered treasonous under a Constitution designed to preserve the power of the rich under the guise of "democracy". The true revolutionary is always a traitor to the established system. The revolutionary, however, always shows steadfast dedication to the well-being of the people. They never rest on laurels nor suffer the laurel wreath to be placed upon their heads. They leap down off of pedestals and wade into the muck of life. They describe the horizon of possibility long before others dare to look in the direction of the rising sun. They dare to call for change when the time for change has come.

It is time for a Constitution 2.0.

Rise and Resist

The Time Is Up; The Time Is Now

Essay Forty-Two

The time is up. The time is now. Gather the people to do the work: the healing, transformative, deepening work of building community, solutions, understanding, skills, knowledge, and hope. You must be the one to make a change, to step out of the rutted tracks of the looming train wreck that is our culture. You must have the courage to walk into the wilderness of what you don't know and embrace the solutions that will save our lives.

All quests and hero's journeys begin with this: the yearning for change, the hope of saving graces, and the long shot of wished-for miracles. In each of us, our willingness to make a change begins with equal measures of fear, courage, and purpose rolled into an electric jolt to the soul . . . a spark that launches us toward danger and potential.

Our world will be saved by billions of ordinary heroes and sheroes who decide to do hundreds of humble and extraordinary actions. Hour by hour, minute by minute, we change our world by withdrawing our support, cooperation, and participation from old destructive systems. By making these shifts, we starve the monster we have become. We share with neighbors to dismantle consumer-capitalism. We gather to tell stories and unplug the corporate media. We build solar panels and shut off the switches of fossil fuels. One small action multiplied by millions of people adds up quickly to massive change. One small action done strategically by a small group of people can catalyze a hundred million more.

Change requires that we live differently. All of us must make changes from the most committed activist who knows she must reconnect to her heart; to the average citizen who suspects he could be doing more; to the terrified investors in fossil fuels who must choose between their industry and their planet; and everyone in between. Real change is never handed to us on a silver platter, nor served by powerful people. When suffragette Elizabeth Cady Stanton wanted to vote, she strode into the polling place and cast her ballot. When Rosa Parks wanted to desegregate the Montgomery buses, she sat down and refused to give up her seat. When tribes among the Anishinaabe wanted to use their promised treaty rights, they walked onto the land to hunt, fish, and gather traditional foods and medicines.

All of them faced violence, danger, arrest, and even death. All of them organized, mobilized, struggled, and ultimately prevailed. None of them sat on the couch waiting for the right people to be put into the right offices to do the right thing. Deep, meaningful change is not handed to us. We wrest it out of the unknown and bring it into existence in our lives.

As Thomas Paine wrote, "we have it in our power to begin the world over again." Our actions, day in and day out, shape this ever-evolving world. We are the potter's hands forming the wet clay vessels of our existence. We are the weavers at the loom, casting the threads of our lives through the wool of the world. We are the stone cutter with chisel and hammer, chipping away at the hard realities that block our forward progress. With such power to shape our world comes the responsibility to wield our lives with intention and skill.

If you want change, live differently. But remember, you alone are not enough. One of our changes is that we must work together. We must reach out from our isolated lives. We must join hands with millions and take collective steps toward the future. You cannot go on a hero's journey alone. Not this time. You must ask others – many others, millions of others – to change their lives, too. Ask your family, friends, and colleagues. Use outreach and organizing tools to ask your neighbors, faith communities, and co-workers. Put nonviolent action to work to compel our society to adopt a change for justice. Mobilize to demand that institutions and industries shift their massive resources into systems that are just, fair, sustainable, and non-harming. In this way, our ordinary actions – multiplied by millions – add up to extraordinary change.

Do not wait another minute to change your life. The time is up. The time is now.

Rise and Resist

The Dawn of Tomorrow is Today!

Essay Forty-Three

Look beyond this night of darkness to the dawn of tomorrow. There is a world beyond the apocalypse, a world beyond war, a world of music and dance, a world where the children are laughing and time stretches slowly, where the Earth lives in the hearts, minds, and souls of our people.

There is a world where the gaping wounds of today close into scars, and then those scars heal over and vanish. The crying of the Earth returns to a love song. Lamentations give way to rejoicing. The wealth of the people breaks through the dam of the elite. Fallow fields burst with life. The deserts bloom, fertile. The concrete cracks into green. The roar of destruction falls silent.

The churning smokestacks of today topple like dictators' statues. Pipelines are dismantled and destroyed. The financing of war is diverted into peace. Schools are rebuilt, bridges repaired, and health is restored to us all.

Ignore the false prophets who tell you this vision cannot be! The empowered elite are addicted to the heroin of darkness. They will mutter like the devil, claiming such a world is impossible. They will try to frighten you into their clutches, subdue you with despair, and enslave you to a lifetime of suffering . . . but they have no vision of tomorrow and no hope for humanity. Their only promise is the continued hell of today.

169

My friends, do not believe them! Their world has no future – for them or for us! It is doomed. Its destiny is failure. For thousands of years, from the early invaders until now, their sickened strand of the human family has ruled. Their evolution is parasitic, colonizing, and all consuming. Their mentality is a disease gone viral. The world is infected by their religion of selfishness and greed. They turn our children into cannibals, dogs eating dogs, worshipping the survival of the fittest. The elite sit at the top of the heaving mass of humanity, profiting as we kill each other for their scraps.

They are carrion eaters, vampires of humanity, blood-sucking parasites that will kill us. We are the host, the people and the planet. We must rise up together and stop them.

We must rise nonviolently with the determination of saints. We must rise with the confidence of doctors. We must rise with compassion, as lovers of the world, and we must remove the infection of destruction even from the elite, and return them to the wholeness of human beings. Greed and consumption are diseases of the mind; they are not the truth of our nature. Beware of false prophets who claim that humans are locusts on this Earth. These prophets are infected with the virus, and delusional.

Listen to the people who speak with clarity and vision, the ones who blaze like beacons in the night. These shining lights of truth know the remedy for the sickness. The dawn of our future is rising in their hearts. Their vision is spreading like laughter rippling through a crowd. This darkness, the madness, the greed and destruction . . . it's all a long cosmic joke, and, one-by-one, we are getting to the punch line: *Love!*

Love is the answer, all the saints say, breaking into smiles. Centuries of hate, division, and greed have brought us to the brink of extinction, but love is the remedy that can save us.

Love one another, this Earth, and Life, itself! Love like there will be no tomorrow. Bring each other closer. Cooperate with each other. Join hands and collaborate on your future. Overwhelm the disease of hate with the remedy of love. Forgive, embrace, rejoice, and resolve that every last human being – and the wounds of the Earth – will be remedied by the love in your heart.

Now you know the truth and the truth lives in you. *You* are the herald of the world that is coming. Shout this vision from the rooftops! Sing it as a choir! Chant it in the streets, teach it to the children, proclaim it in halls of power, announce it on the radio, whisper it to each other until it breaks like a wave and crashes through our world, sweeping everywhere like the rising light of day. Live it, walk it, breathe it, be it . . . until the love of tomorrow joins hands with today, and the healing of the world embraces all.

Rise and Resist

About the Author

Rivera Sun is the author of *The Way Between, The Lost Heir, Billionaire Buddha, The Dandelion Insurrection, The Roots of Resistance; and Steam Drills, Treadmills, and Shooting Stars,* as well as theatrical plays, a study guide to nonviolent struggle, three volumes of poetry, and hundreds of articles. She has red hair, a twin sister, and a fondness for esoteric mystics. She went to Bennington College to study writing as a Harcourt Scholar and graduated with a degree in dance. She lives in an earthship house in New Mexico, where she writes essays and novels. She is a trainer in strategy for nonviolent movements and an activist. Rivera has been an aerial dancer, a bike messenger, and a gung-fu style tea server. Everything else about her - except her writing - is perfectly ordinary.

Rivera Sun also loves hearing from her readers:
Email: info@riverasun.com
Website: http://www.riverasun.com/
Facebook: https://www.facebook.com/rivera.sun.3
Twitter: @RiveraSunAuthor

Praise for Rivera Sun's
The Dandelion Insurrection

"A rare gem of a book, a must read, it charts the way forward in this time of turmoil and transformation." - **Velcrow Ripper, director Occupy Love, Genie Award Winner**

"When fear is used to control us, love is how we rebel!" Under a gathering storm of tyranny, Zadie Byrd Gray whirls into the life of Charlie Rider and asks him to become the voice of the Dandelion Insurrection. With the rallying cry of life, liberty, and love, Zadie and Charlie fly across America leaving a wake of revolution in their path. Passion erupts. Danger abounds. The lives of millions hang by a thin thread of courage, but in the midst of the madness, the golden soul of humanity blossoms . . . and miracles start to unfold!

"This novel will not only make you want to change the world, it will remind you that you can." - **Gayle Brandeis, author of** *The Book of Dead Birds*, **winner of the Bellwether Prize for Socially Engaged Fiction**

"In a world where despair has deep roots, *The Dandelion Insurrection* bursts forth with joyful abandon." - **Medea Benjamin, Co-founder of CodePink**

"THE handbook for the coming revolution!" - **Lo Daniels, Editor of Dandelion Salad**

174

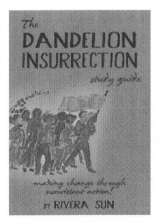

Praise For Rivera Sun's
The Roots of Resistance

"If you loved Starhawk's *Fifth Sacred Thing*, if you loved recently-departed Ursula K. LeGuin's *The Dispossessed*, if you admire the spirit of the Standing Rock Water Protectors, you will drink in this must-read page-turner . . . an epic story that will move your spirit, bringing tears to your eyes and healing to your soul." - **Rosa Zubizarreta, Author of** *From Conflict to Creative Collaboration*

"A tale of revolution, resistance and the indomitable power of love . . . skims tantalizingly close to the surface of what could be political reality in these United States in just a few short years. Recommended for wanderers, whistleblowers, and anyone curious about the question of violence vs. nonviolence." - **Elizabeth Murray, former Deputy National Intelligence Officer for the Near East, National Intelligence Council and Member in Residence, Ground Zero Center for Nonviolent Action**

"*The Roots of Resistance* is a compelling page-turner about the inner workings of a nonviolent movement and how it deals with forces that try to sabotage it. I loved this book!" - **Judy Olson, Backbone Campaign**

"This book is a treasure of a resource; it's a repertoire of nonviolence techniques disguised as a novel." - **Michael Nagler, Founder and President, The Metta Center for Nonviolence**

176

"A must-read, written by the talented Rivera Sun! Resistance is essential, as nonviolent actions will save humanity. Amazingly inspirational!" - **Robin Wildman, Nonviolent Schools**

"Billed as 'Book Two of the Dandelion Trilogy,' this one makes me hope Sun is punching out Book Three soon and perhaps, like Douglas Adams, will give us, someday, Books Four and Five of the Trilogy." - **Tom H. Hastings, Conflict Resolution Assistant Professor, Portland State University**

"This novel is a nuanced political, moral, and emotional exploration of risks, sacrifices and rewards that a commitment to social justice can elicit in the hearts of some extraordinary people. I was frequently moved to resist the plot's incessant pull of haste so that I might linger and relish the rich emotional dynamics within such noble characters. A memorable cognitive and emotional journey."
- **Nim Batchelor, Professor of Philosophy, Elon University**

"Rivera Sun always gifts us with usefully creative fiction. Her *Roots of Resistance* - the second novel of her Dandelion Trilogy - offers an inspiring story to help guide love-based strategic change efforts . . . . It takes a storyteller like Rivera Sun who inspires us to rise to the challenge as her characters do, because her stories tell us how."
- **Tom Atlee, Co-Intelligence Institute**

"Rivera Sun's *The Roots of Resistance* tells a story of a creative nonviolent resistance that is transforming the United States from inequality to equality, democratic dictatorship to a real

people's democracy, to a United States that puts necessities of the people and protection of the planet before profits. The resisters from *The Dandelion Insurrection*, the first story in this three-part series, fight the challenges of infiltration, misdirection and media propaganda that activists face today. They show us how to respond and the difficulties these challenges cause within movements. They also give us hope of what could be in a way that seems achievable."
- **Kevin Zeese and Margaret Flowers, Popular Resistance**

"Rivera has crafted a vision of an unstoppable movement for democracy and leaves no corner or controversy of nonviolence unexplored. Find yourself within these pages and learn some new techniques for action while you're here."
- **Stephanie N. Van Hook, Executive Director, The Metta Center for Nonviolence**

"In times of despair, we need hope. In times of frustration, we need inspiration. In times of confusion, we need clarity. Rivera brings us all of these and more."
- **Stephen Zunes, University of San Francisco**

"Once again Rivera Sun weaves a captivating story of change and shows us a path forward out of the fear and control of our current chaotic world and toward a world whose foundation is Love. This is just the story we need to inform, inspire and call us forth into action." - **Cindy Reinhardt, the Success Zone**

All of Rivera's books are available at her website www.RiveraSun.com and everywhere books are sold.

Made in the USA
Middletown, DE
12 October 2020

21721425R00116